A STRAIGHT
GUIDE TO
COMPANY LAW

Andrew Pierce

Straightforward Publishing

www.straightforwardco.co.uk

Straightforward Publishing

British Library Cataloguing in Publication Data. A Catalogue record for this book is available from the British Library.

ISBN
978-1-84716-698-2

Printed by 4edge www.4edge.co.uk
Cover Design by Bookworks Islington

CONTENTS

****

INTRODUCTION

A Straightforward Guide to Company Law, updated to 2017, is intended to cover all the main points of company law, in a way which will be of use to the layperson and the professional, as well as the student.

Company law is very complex and the average person, particularly the person engaged in business, has only a vague idea of these complexities. The law tends to become ever more complex in relation to public limited companies.

The book covers the nature of a company, company finance, company management, company meetings and the protection of shareholders along with liquidation of companies and reconstructions and takeovers. It is therefore comprehensive in its approach.

For many years, the main Act regulating companies was the 1948 Companies Act. There were a number of subsequent Companies Acts. The passage of the 2006 Companies Act has superseded the 1985 Companies Act and is now the main reference point. In addition, there is reference to the 1986 Insolvency Act and the Statutory instruments flowing from that Act, specifically the 1986 Insolvency Rules and also the 2002 Enterprise Act.

In addition, the Small Business, Enterprise and Employment Act 2015 has changed the way companies report, and also certain shareholdings, which will be outlined fully in Chapter 4.

It is hoped that this brief introduction to company law will be of use to all who read it and that it sheds some light on the law and subsequent internal administration of a company, whether a private, limited, or public limited company.

****

Chapter 1

The Nature of a Company

When people set up a business they will usually form a (limited) company or a partnership. The main distinction between a company and a partnership is that the company is treated as a separate entity, or person in law. The partnership, on the other hand is not seen as a separate entity and consists only of those who have chosen to join together for business purposes.

One other crucial distinction is that a company will pay corporation tax, whilst a partnership will pay only that tax due as an individual liability.

A company has access to what is known as "limited liability". This is where the liability for debt of directors is limited. Not all companies are limited companies. If a company is not limited there is no requirement to file accounts at Companies House. Partnerships have no such access to limited liability.

A company can separate ownership from control. People who subscribe to a company and purchase its shares do not necessarily have any control over the company or a hand in running the business. This is especially the case in a large Public Limited

Company, where shareholders receive a return on their investment in the company.

A further distinction and advantage for a company is in the area of raising finance. The company as a separate entity can raise finance in its own right, mortgage any assets by way of a floating charge, and generally enjoy access to finance that is not available to a partnership.

Public companies and private companies

Another main area which runs through company law is that of the distinction between the public company and the private company. The majority of companies in the United Kingdom are private companies. One main feature of company law is that, with a few exceptions, the same rules apply to private companies as to public companies.

The second EC directive on company law did, however, lead to modifications to company law, with distinctions being drawn between public and private companies, these being incorporated into the Companies Act 2006.

One main feature of a public company is that it must have a minimum subscribed share capital of at least £50,000, or its equivalent in Euros paid up to at least 25 percent before it can be incorporated (s586 of the CA 2006). The second EC directive sets out the regulations for this, with the minimum subscribed share capital for public companies within the EU being £25,000 ECU. In addition to the payment of the minimum subscribed share capital to at least 25 percent on initial allotment of shares, the whole of any premium must be paid up.

A further distinction between public and private companies is in the name of the company. The Companies Act of 2006 states that a public company must end with suffix "public limited company" or the abbreviation PLC. In Wales the term is cwmni cyhoeddus cyfyngedig with the abbreviation ccc. A private company will end with the term "limited" or the Welsh equivalent cyfyngedig or "cyf".

In addition, another fundamental distinction between the public and private company is that the private company is prohibited from seeking finance from the public by offering shares or debentures. The public company is authorised to seek shares in this way.

It is worth noting that most public companies are not listed-as of January 2016 there were 6,271 public companies of which only 2,329 were listed. Listed companies have to comply with more and more regulations. Currently, in addition to complying with the companies Act 2006, listed companies are also required to comply with the provisions of Pt V1 of the Financial Services and Markets Act 2000 and a body of rules collectively known as the Listing Regime, which principally consists of (i) The Disclosures and Transparency Rules (ii) the Prospectus Rules and most importantly (iii) The Listing Rules. These latter rules are drafted and administered by the Financial Conduct Authority and impose obligations upon listed companies in relation to the disclosure of information, as well as supplementing the CA 2006 as regards certain areas of internal control. These rules have the force of law as the FCA is regarded as the 'competent authority' under part V1 of the Financial Services and Markets Act 2000.

Company limited by guarantee

A company limited by guarantee is private company, very like a private company limited by shares, but it does not have a share capital. It is widely used for charities, clubs, community enterprises and some co-operatives. The vast majority of such companies are non-profit distributing, but they do not have to be.

A company limited by guarantee is registered at Companies House, has articles of association, directors, etc., and is subject to all the requirements of the Companies Acts (except those relating to shares). There are no shares and so no shareholders, but such a company does have members, who meet and control the company through general meetings. The directors are often called a management committee or council of management, etc. but in law are still company directors and subject to all the rules that affect other directors.

A company limited by guarantee confers limited liability as effectively as a company limited by shares. The articles state that the members guarantee to pay its debts, but only up to a fixed amount each. Usually that sum is £1, and no member can be liable for more than that amount if the company fails. The Companies Act 2006 also outlines other distinctions between companies:

- A private company can operate with one director, in contrast to the public company which is required to have two

- A private company needs only to have one member whereas a public company has to have two (s154 CA 2006).

- The company secretary of a private company can be anyone and that person needs no particular qualifications. There is now no legal requirement for a company secretary of a private company under the CA 2006. The company secretary of a public company must be qualified, holding a recognised qualification in this area in order to hold the post.

- Before a public company can pay a dividend, it must ensure that it has trading profits and that its capital assets are maintained in value to at least the value of the subscribed share capital plus undistributable reserves. There is no such rule applying to a private company (CA 2006)

- Before a public company can distribute shares in exchange for property it must obtain an independent experts valuation of the property. This requirement does not apply to a private company (CA 2006)

- A public company may not issue shares in exchange for services. This rule does not apply to a private company (CA 2006).

14

- The Directors of a public company must call an Extraordinary General Meeting (EGM) if it suffers a serious loss of capital. There is no requirement for a private company to do this.

- Proxies in a private company may speak at a meeting. In a public company there is no such right.

- In a private company, there are courses of action, which may be taken in order to dispense with formalities such as the need to hold an Annual General Meeting, the laying of accounts and the annual appointment of auditors. This is not the case with a public company, which is rigidly bound.

- Private companies may act by unanimous written resolution, in most cases. This does not apply to public companies.

- Where there is a proposal to elect a director aged 70 or over to the board of a public company, special notice is required. There is no such requirement for a private company.

- The minimum age for a company director under the CA 2006 s s57, for both private and public companies is 16.

Limited Liability Partnerships

Under the Limited Liability Partnerships Act 2000, it is possible to create a different form of business association called a limited liability partnership. Under the LLPA 2000, a LLP becomes a corporate body with a legal personality separate from that of its members. It follows therefore that members of a LLP will not normally become liable for the debts of the LLP. The law relating to ordinary partnerships does not relate to a LLP.

Many of the detailed provisions relating to LLP's are to be found in secondary legislation, in particular the Limited Partnership Regulations 2001. These regulations apply some of the provisions of the CA 2006 and the Insolvency Act 1986 to LLP's with some modifications to reflect the different nature of an LLP.

Formation of an LLP

An LLP is created by registration with the registrar of companies. Once the registrar has registered an LLP and issued a certificate of incorporation, a new corporate body with a separate legal personality of its own is created. Section 2 (1) of the LPA 2000 provides that:

Two or more persons associated for carrying on a lawful business with a view to profit must have subscribed their names to an incorporation document which is to be delivered to the registrar of companies.

Community Interest Companies

The Companies (Audit, Investigations and Community Enterprise) Act 2004 and regulations made under the Act, establish the legislative framework for CICs. CICs are regulated by the CIC Regulator.

A Community Interest Company can be registered in England and Wales, Scotland or Northern Ireland. It is a hybrid between a charity and a profit making company. A Community Interest Company must be set up and run for the benefit of the community. A CIC can only be registered with the consent of the Community Interest Companies Regulator. The application must comply with CIC legislation as well as the usual rules for registration of a company. The CIC Regulator has to be satisfied that the proposed company is being set up to benefit the community and that its articles include all the provisions required of a community interest company. Each year, the CIC must submit a return stating what its activities have been and that these have been of community benefit.

Property management companies

A property management company in England and Wales, Scotland or Northern Ireland is a particular type of company: one set up to hold an interest in a property which is divided into units, each unit being owned separately. A typical example is a large house which has been divided into a number of flats (sometimes called a flat management company), each flat being owned by one or two people. Such a company can also be used for large blocks of flats, housing estates and commercial properties divided into units. A property management company will always be a private limited company. It may be limited by shares or limited by guarantee. People who deal with property management companies professionally tend to have their preferences. It is one of those circumstances where either type of company will work perfectly well. The only significant difference between them is that a company limited by shares has a share capital, owned by its shareholders and a company limited by guarantee does not, but is controlled by its shareholders. If the company is to own the freehold, some people prefer it to be a company limited by shares as this gives a form of ownership between the shareholders (who own the company) and the property (which is owned by the company). On the other hand, with a company limited by guarantee, there is no need to transfer a share when the flat is sold.

The concept of the corporate personality

The principle of the separate legal personality of a company was established in an important case, Saloman v A Saloman (1897). The facts of the case were that Saloman had incorporated his shoe repair business, transferring it to a company. He took all the shares of the company with the exception of six which were held by his wife, daughter and four sons. Part of the payment for transfer of the business was made in the form of debentures (secured loan) issued by the company to Saloman. Saloman transferred the debentures to Broderip in exchange for a loan. Saloman defaulted on payment of interest on the loan and Broderip sought to enforce the security against the company. Unsecured creditors tried to put the company into liquidation. There was a dispute between Broderip and the unsecured creditors over who had priority over payment of the debt. It was argued for the creditors that Salmons security was void as the company was a sham and was in reality the agent of Salomon.

The House of Lords held that this was not the case as the company had been properly incorporated and therefore the security was valid and could be enforced. This case is seen as one of the most important cases in company law as it is from this that many principles of company law flow. There are certain statutory exceptions to the Salmon principle and they are as follows:

- Section 7 of the Companies Act 2006 provides that if the membership of a public company falls below the statutory minimum of two then the remaining member should after a period of six months grace, be liable for the company's debts and obligations where he or she knew of the situation.

- Section 767 (3) of the Companies Act 2006 provides that where a public company fails to obtain a trading certificate in addition to its certificate of incorporation before trading and borrowing money then the companies directors are liable for any obligations incurred.

- Sections 398-408 of the Companies Act 2006 provides that where a group situation exists (i.e. where there is a holding company and subsidiaries) then group accounts should be prepared. In assessing whether this is the case, clearly the veil is being lifted to see if the holding company/subsidiary relationship exists.

- Section 83 of the Companies Act 2006 provides that if a company officer misdescribes the company in a letter, bill, invoice, order, receipt or any other document then the officer is liable in the event of the obligation not being honored.

- Section 994 of the Companies Act 2006 may involve lifting the veil to determine, for example, the basis on which the company was formed.

- Sections 1159-1160 of the Companies Act 2006 set out the formula for determining if a holding company/subsidiary company relationship exists.

- Section 15 of the Company Directors Disqualification Act 1986 provides that if a director who is disqualified continues to act, he or she will be personally liable for the debts and obligations of the company.

- Section 122 (1) (g) of the Insolvency Act 1986 provides that a petitioner may present a petition to wind up a company on the just and equitable ground.

- On occasion, this may be based on a situation involving the lifting of the company veil in order to determine the basis of the company formation.

- Section 213 of the Insolvency Act 1986 provides that where a person trades through the medium of a company, knowing that the company is unable to pay its debts, he or she may be held liable for contributions to the companies assets where the company is being wound up. This has a criminal counterpart in s999 (1) of the CA 2006.

- Section 6 of the Law of Property Act 1969 provides that where a person has a controlling interest in a company which is carrying on a business, the business is treated as the controller for the purposes of refusing a renewal of a tenancy issued out of the Landlord and Tenant Act 1954.

In addition to the statutory exceptions to the Salomon principle there are certain judicial decisions which have had an impact. One such decision is that of combating fraud. There are several well-known legal cases that have dealt with fraud.

One such case is that of Jones v Lipman (1962) where a vendor decided to sell a piece of land and then changed his mind. This resulted in the would-be purchaser suing for specific performance. In order to avoid this, the vendor transferred the piece of land to a company. The courts held that although the company was another legal entity nevertheless the action was designed to avoid legal action and the courts refused to accept the action of transferring the land and ordered specific performance against the vendor.

Therefore the action of transferring assets from the individual to a company in order to change a legal status is not tolerated if it is seen as fraudulent, as in the case above. There are numerous other examples of a company veil being lifted in order to combat fraud.

Group structures

Group structures are governed by s1159 of the CA 2006. Sometimes the fact that a company is within a group is seen as a reason for identifying it with another company within the group. In Harold Holdsworth and Co (Wakefield) Ltd v Caddies (1955) the respondent held an employment contract with the appellant company to serve it as managing director. The House of Lords held that the appellant company could require the respondent to serve a subsidiary company.

A fundamental case in this area is DHN Food Distributors Ltd v Tower Hamlets London Borough Council (1976). This case concerned compensation for compulsory purchase. The company operating the business was the holding company and the premises were owned by the companies wholly owned subsidiary. Compensation was only payable for disturbance to the companies business if the business was operated on land owned by the company.

In this case, Lord Denning said:

"In many respects a group of companies are treated together for the purposes of accounts, they are treated as one concern. This is especially the case when a parent company owns all the shares of the subsidiary-so much so that it can control the activities of the subsidiaries. These subsidiaries are bound hand and foot and must do just what the parent company says."

Companies and crimes and negligence

Companies, as any individual, can commit crimes, although there are certain obvious exceptions, such as rape or murder. A company can, however, commit manslaughter. In December 1994, OLL Limited became the first company in England to be convicted of manslaughter. This arose from the death of four young people in a canoeing accident in Lyme Bay which was organised by the company.

In the case, Kite v OLL Ltd the managing director of the company that organised the trip was imprisoned for manslaughter and the company fined £60,000.

The Law Commission reported on the law of corporate manslaughter in consultation paper no 135 (1994). They recommended a new offence based on whether the companies conduct fell significantly below what could reasonably be expected of it in the context of the significant risk of death or injury of which it should have been aware. In a later report (Law Commission Paper no 237) Legislating the Criminal Code, Involuntary Manslaughter

(1996) the Law Commission, in its final report, called for a new offence of corporate killing comparable to killing by gross negligence. It is imperative that at least one person should be recognised and identified as the directing force of the company causing death by gross negligence when acting as the company.

In the only other case of a company being convicted of manslaughter, Jackson Transport (Ossett) Ltd. The company concerned was a medium sized company employing about 40 people. A person was killed in May 1994 while he was cleaning behind a tanker containing chemicals. Mr Jackson, the owner, ran the business himself and he and the company was convicted of manslaughter.

Companies may also commit strict liability offences. This is important in areas such as pollution and food safety. There is however, a diligence defence and if the company can demonstrate the practice of diligence, or that lack of diligence was on the part of a person who was not the true embodiment of the company, it will escape liability.

Now read the key points from Chapter One overleaf.

****

Key points from Chapter One

- A company is treated as a separate entity, or person, in law.

- The Companies Act 2006 is the main body of law governing the activities of companies

- A company has limited liability. This is where the liability for debts of directors is limited.

- A Company can separate ownership from control. This is especially the case in large public limited companies.

- One main feature of a public company is that it must have a minimum subscribed share capital of at least £50,000.

- Private companies are prohibited from raising share capital from the public.

- There are other important distinctions between public and private companies.

- Companies can commit, and be tried, for crimes such as manslaughter.

Chapter 2

The Constitution of a Company

Under the Companies Act 2006, the importance of a company's memorandum of association has been reduced to a mere historical record. Constitutional provisions are to be contained within the Articles of Association instead. The memorandum is a document that needs to be submitted as part of the incorporation process and will not be capable of amendment. The information that was contained within the memorandum will now be provided to the registrar in an application for registration under s 9 of the Companies Act 2006.

The application for registration must contain the following::

- The name of the company (s9) (2) of the Companies Act 2006.
- If the company is a public company a statement indicating this s 9(2).

A statement that the registered office of the company is situated in England and Wales, in Wales or in Scotland s9 (7).
The application must also contain:

- A statement of initial shareholding
- A Statement of share capital
- A Statement of guarantee
- A Statement of proposed officers
- A Statement of compliance

Objects clauses and *ultra vires*

By virtue of s 31 of the CA 2006 unless a company's articles specifically restrict the objects of the company, its objects are unrestricted. If the company does decide to amend its objects, then this change must be made by amendment to the articles. The new law is stated in s 40 of the CA 2006. The effect of the new law is to effectively abolish *ultra vires*. However, there are still occasions where a challenge could arise. These are where a director or connected person is involved or a third party acted in bad faith. A Challenge could also arise if an injunction is sought to prevent directors acting or to allege a breach of duty after events. S 239 of the CA 2006 now only requires ordinary resolutions to ratify any breaches of duty by directors. However, the votes of any director or person involved in the breach of duty will not count. S 41 (3) of the CA 2006 makes any directors involved liable to account for the transaction and to indemnify the company whether they knew they were exceeding their powers or not.

The position at common law

The old case will still be applicable in certain limited circumstances. Prior to statutory reform, at common law, contracts that were outside the scope of the company's objects were held to be *ultra vires* and void.

Before statutory intervention therefore the question was simple: if the objects clause covered the relevant contract it was valid. If it was outside the scope of the company's permitted range of activities it was void and unenforceable.

There are several cases which serve to highlight the nature of the above. One such case is that of Payne and Co Ltd (1904) where a company borrowed money which was then used for purposes outside of the objects of the company. The lender was able to enforce the loan because he did not know the purpose of the loan.

In Re John Beauforte Ltd (1953) a different decision was reached on the basis that a supplier to the company provided coke. The company could have been using the coke for internal purposes as it was engaged in the manufacturer of veneered panels. The order was placed on notepaper showing that the company was engaged in this business and the courts held that the combination of constructive notice of what the company could do and the actual notice of what it was doing was fatal to the suppliers claim.

Statutory intervention

Article 9 of the first EC directive on company law provided as follows:

- Acts done by the organs of the company shall be binding upon it even if those acts are not within the objects of the company, unless such acts exceed powers that the law confers or allows to be conferred on those organs.

Since that first article, company law has developed and now the Companies Act 2006 has amended the law on ultra vires and objects clauses.

The Prentice Report (reform of the ultra vires rule, a consultative document (1986) (par 50) put forward the following recommendations in relation to the reform of the ultra vires rule:

- A company should have the capacity to do any act whatsoever
- A third party dealing with the company should not be affected by the contents of any document merely because it is registered with the registrar of companies or with the company.
- A company should be bound by the acts of its board or an individual director.
- The third party should be under no obligation to determine the scope of the authority of a company's board or individual

director, or the contents of the company's articles or memorandum.

- A third party who has actual knowledge that a board or an individual director do not possess the authority to enter into a transaction on behalf of the company should not be allowed to enforce against the company but the company should be free to ratify this. The same result should obtain where a third party has knowledge that the transaction falls outside of the company's objects, but in this case ratification should be by a special resolution.

- Knowledge in this context will require understanding, and it will only be the knowledge of the individual entering into the particular transaction that will be relevant

- The proposal (in relation to third parties) should be modified where a third party is an officer or director of the company and in this situation constructive knowledge should be sufficient to render the transaction unenforceable and for this purpose constructive knowledge should mean the type of knowledge which may reasonably be expected of a person carrying out the functions of that director or officer of the company.

- In consequence of the recommendations of the Prentice Report the Companies Act of 1989 amended the law on ultra vires and objects clauses.

The Companies act of 2006, provides that the validity of an act done by a company shall not be called into question on the ground of lack of capacity by reason of anything in the company's memorandum. A transaction can thus be enforced by an outsider or the company.

A member may, however, restrain the company from entering into a transaction which is outside the company's objects. This power to restrain the company can only operate where the company has not entered into a binding transaction to perform the act.

If the directors exceed limitations on their powers then they are in breach of their director's duties. Even if the directors conclude a contract outside of the objects clause, and a member has not succeeded in restraining this, the company may be able to sue their directors for breach of duties (Companies Act 2006). It is open to the company to ratify what has been done by special resolution. The company may also ratify by a separate special resolution the breach of the director's duties thereby putting the matter outside of litigation.

S.40 (1) of the CA now provides that where a person deals with a company in good faith the power of the directors to bind the company shall be deemed to be free of any limitation under the company's constitution. The outsider is not to be regarded as in bad faith by reason only by his knowing that the transaction was outside of the director's powers.

Further, this section provides that:

...a party to any transaction with a company is not bound to enquire as to whether it is permitted by the companies memorandum or as to any limitations on the board of directors to bind the company or to authorise others to do so.

The wording under sections s.40 (1) will protect outsiders in most circumstances. The CA 2006 builds on these provisions, which extends to other officers acting on behalf of the company.

This provides that:

... a person shall not be taken to have notice of any such matters merely because of its being disclosed in any document kept by the registrar of companies (and thus available for inspection) or made available by the company for inspection.

The rules governing company names

The first clause in the company's memorandum should be the name of that company. The statutory provisions relating to company names are set out in The Companies Act 2006. These provisions are as follows:

- Section 58 of the CA 2006 provides that the name of a public company must end with the word "PLC" or the Welsh equivalent as mentioned. A private company limited by shares or guarantee should end with "Limited" or the abbreviation Ltd or the Welsh equivalent as mentioned.

- In certain cases, a private limited company may be permitted to omit the word "limited" from the end of its name. The Companies Act 2006 permits companies to omit the word limited on satisfying certain conditions. The company concerned must be a private limited company and have as its objects the promotion of science, commerce, art, education, religion, charity or any profession and anything incidental or conductive to any of these objects and must have a requirement in its constitution that its profits or other income be applied in promoting these objects. The constitution must also prohibit the payment of dividends to its members and require all of the assets which would otherwise be available to its members generally to be transferred on its winding up to another body with similar objects or to a body the objects of which are the promotion of charity and anything incidental.

- Section 53 of the Companies Act 2006 prohibits the use of certain names. The words public limited company, limited and unlimited can only be used at the end of a company name as may be the Welsh equivalents.

- The name must not be the same as a name already registered at Companies House. (s 66 CA 2006)

S 55 of the CA 2006 states that there are certain words and expressions, which require the prior permission of either the Secretary for State or some other designated body.. There is a list of the words specified in regulations made under s55 of the Companies Act. If the name of the company implies some regional, national or international pre-eminence, governmental link or sponsorship or some pre-eminent status, then consent may be required.

- The choice of company name is limited by other considerations. If the name is a registered trademark the person who owns the trademark may take action to prevent the use of the name under the Trades Mark Act 1994.
- The use of a name which is already used by an existing business (whether sole trader, partnership or company) or a name which is similar to that of an existing business such that it appears to the public that there is a link between the two businesses may be subject to legal action, such as an injunction to restrain the company from further use.

Change of name

Section 77 (1) of the Companies Act 2006 provides that a company may change its name by special resolution in general meeting. There are other provisions relating to change of name, that is if the Secretary of State or Companies House gives a direction that the company must do this. This will usually happen in a situation where the original name was misleading or that the name itself is deemed to be of potential harm.

The articles of association of a company

The articles of association is now the most important document to be submitted to the registrar (CA 2006 s 18). the articles tend to regulate the internal workings of the company and typically cover such issues as the balance of power between the members and the directors, the conduct of general meetings, and certain issues pertaining to shares and distribution of assets.

Although a company must have articles of association, the contents of the articles are not laid down by the 2006 CA. Under s 20 of the 2006 CA, a limited company doesn't have to register articles. If they are not registered then model articles drafted under the Companies (Model Articles) Regulations can be adopted. Section 21 of the Companies Act 2006 allows a company to alter its articles by special resolution. However, the power to alter the articles of a company is restricted by the following:

- The company cannot alter its articles in a way which would lead to contravention of the 2006 Companies Act.
- Any alteration of the company's articles which would lead to a difference between, or a clash between the memorandum is void.

- If an alteration of the articles is proposed which conflicts with an order of the court then this would be automatically void.

- If the proposed alteration of the articles leads to an alteration of the class rights then special procedures need to be followed in addition to a special resolution being passed. A company must follow a regime which is appropriate to the variation of class rights which is set out in s121 of the 2006 Companies Act.

If a change of articles involves a variation of class rights then this procedure must be followed. If a company has more than one class of shares then questions of variations of class rights sometimes arise. Once it has been determined that there is more than one class of share in the company then the next question for determination is whether there has been a variation of rights attached to those shares. Once it has been established that there has been a variation of class rights then the rules that have to be followed to carry the variation into effect are dependent upon whether the company has a share capital or not. If the company has a share capital then the rights may be varied:

a) in accordance with provision in the company's articles for the variation of those rights; or

b) where the company's articles contain no such provision, if the members of that class consent to the variation in accordance with this section.

The consent required for the purposes of this section on the part of the members of a class is-

a) consent in writing from at least three quarters of the members of the class, or

b) a special resolution passed at a separate general meeting of the members of that class sanctioning the variation.

If class rights are varied, dissentient minorities have special rights to object to the alteration. They must satisfy certain conditions. The dissenters must hold no less than 15% of the issued shares of the class and must not have voted in favour of the resolution (s 633 of the CA 2006). They may then object to the variation within 21 days of consent being given to the resolution.

If the class rights are varied under a procedure set out in the memorandum or articles of association of the company or if the class rights are set out otherwise than in the memorandum or articles are silent on variation, then dissentient minorities have special rights to object to the alteration.

They must satisfy certain conditions:

- The dissenters must hold no less than 15 percent of the issued shares of the class and must not have voted in favour of the resolution. They may then object to the variation within 21 days of the consent being given to the resolution. On occasions, their objections may be upheld by the courts (s 623 CA 2006).

'Bona Fide for the benefit of the company as a whole'

In addition to the various statutory restrictions considered above, the power to alter a company's articles is subject to the overriding principle that any alteration must be bona fide for the benefit of the company as a whole. One case that illustrates this is Allen v Gold Reefs of West Africa Limited (1900). In this case, the company's articles originally provided:

.....that the company shall have a first and paramount lien for all debts obligations and liabilities of any member to and towards the company upon all shares (not being fully paid) held by such member...........

The alteration proposed was to delete the words 'not being fully paid' to provide the company with a lien over any shares of a member where a debt was due from that member. The alteration was challenged. Lindley MR said as follows:

Wide, however, as the language of s 50 is (now section 21 of the CA 2006) the power conferred by it must, like all other powers, be exercised subject to those general principles of law and equity which are applicable to all powers conferred on majorities and enabling

38

them to bind minorities stock. It must be exercised not only in the manner required by the law, but also bona fide for the benefit of the company as a whole, and it must not be exceeded. These conditions are always implied and are seldom, if ever, expressed. But, if they are complied with, I can discover no grounds for judicially putting other restrictions on the power conferred by the section and those contained within it.

In the instant case the Court of Appeal held that the power had been exercised *bona fide*.

The constitution as a contract

The courts have long held that a companies articles form a contract between a company and its members, and between the members themselves as in the case Tavarone Mining Co (Pritchards Case) 1873. Section 33(1) of the CA 2006 expands upon this by stating that:

The provisions of a company's constitution binds the company and its members to the same extent as if they were covenants on the part of the company and of each member to observe those provisions.

Accordingly, the company's constitution forms what is known as the 'statutory contract' and imposes obligations upon:

- the company when dealing with its members
- the members when dealing with the company
- the members when dealing with each other.

The statutory contract

the statutory contract created by s33 is unusual in that differs from a standard contract and is not subject to standard contractual rules. One cardinal rules that does apply to the statutory contract is the doctrine of privity of contract The stautory contract is formed between a company and its members-persons not party to the contract are therefore not permitted to enforce the rules of the constitution. One case that demonstrates this is Eley v Positive Government Security Life Assurance Co (1876) where Eley, a solicitor drafted the defendant company articles, which were then registered. the articles provided that Eley would act as the company solicitor and could not be removed unless guilty of misconduct. Soon after, the company ceased to employ Eley and employed another solicitor and Eley alleged that the company had breached the terms of contract. Eley lost the case as Eley was not party to the statutory contract and therefore could not sue.

The contract between the company and its members

As the constitution forms a contract between the company and its members, it follows that both parties can enforce compliance with the terms of the constitution against the other. In the case of Hickman v Kent or Romney Marsh Sheepbreeders Association (1915) the company's articles provided that any dispute between it and a member should be referred for arbitration before any legal proceedings were initiated. The company purported to expel one of its members (Hickman) from its organisation but, instead of referring the dispute to arbitration, Hickman petitioned the High Court for an injunction restraining his expulsion.

It was held that the articles formed a contract between the company and its members. The company was therefore permitted to enforce the term of the articles and require disputes to be referred to arbitration. the High Court stayed Hickmans legal proceedings and he was subsequently expelled.

Member enforcing compliance of a term of the constitution

A member can enforce compliance of a term of the constitution against the company, as occurred in the case of Pender v Lushington (1877) where the company's articles provided that its members would have one vote for every ten shares up to a maximum of 100 votes. Consequently, members with over 1,000 shares would not have voting power commensurate to their shares. To avoid this, members with over 1,000 shares (of which Pender was one) transferred some of their excess shares to several nominees, thereby unlocking the votes within them. the company's chairman

(Lushington) refused to accept the nominees votes and Pender alleged that his votes were improperly rejected.

Penders action succeeded The shares were properly transferred and registered to nominees so refusing to accept their votes constituted a breach of the articles.

It is important to note that not all the terms of the constitution can be enforced this way. As Buckley LJ stated in Blagood v Henderson's Transvaal Estates Ltd (1908) , 'the purpose of the constitution is to define the position of the shareholder as shareholder and not to bind him in his capacity as an individual'.

The contract between members themselves

Just as the constitution forms a contract between the company and its members , so too does it form a contract amongst the members themselves. Accordingly, a breach of the statutory contract by a member can be enforced by another member, providing that the provision breached concerns a members rights.

In the case Rayfield v hands (1960) the company's articles provided that, if a member wished to sell his shares, he should inform the directors, who would then purchase the shares between them. Rayfield wished to sell his shares and so notified the directors, but the directors refused to purchase his shares. the directors were all members of the company, and so Rayfield sought an order requiring the directors to purchase his shares.

the court ordered that the directors should purchase Rayfields shares. As the company was a quasi partnership, the article provision affected the directors in their capacity as members. Accordingly, the provision concerned a membership right and formed part of the statutory contract.

The capacity of a company

As the company is a legal person, it can enter into contracts in much the same way as natural persons can. However, historically, the company's ability to enter into contracts was subject to a significant limitation. prior to the passing of the CA 2006, all companies were required to state in their memorandathe objects or purposes for which the company was set up (this is known as the 'objects clause') the objects clause serves to limit the contractual capacity of the company and if a company entered into a contract that was outside the scope of its objects clause, the company would be acting *ultra vires* (beyond ones powers) and the contract would be void.

This restriction on a company's capacity was introduced to protect a person who provided a company with capital, namely members and creditors. Such persons provided capital on the expectation that the company would pursue lines of business for which it was set up and not for activities outside of the company's remit.

The abolition of the requirement to include an objects clause

the requirement of an objects clause has been abolished by the CA 2006 (although companies can still include an objects clause if they wish and such companies will accordingly have unrestricted objects (CA 2006 s 31.(1). For those companies incorporated before the passing of the CA 2006 a special resolution by company members can delete existing objects clauses, thereby acquiring unrestricted capacity

Alteration of the articles

As a company, or the markets that it operates in evolves , it may be necessary for it to alter its articles. Section 21 (1) of the CA 2006 provides that a company may amend its articles by passing a special resolution and, in certain cases, the courts also have the power to amend the articles. However, it should be noted that the ability to alter the articles is not limitless and both statute and common law impose restrictions on a company's ability to alter its articles.

Entrenched article provisions

A company cannot make its articles unalterable (Walker v London Tramways co (1879). However, the CA 2006 s.22 introduced the ability to entrench company article provisions, making it more difficult to alter. This could be done by requiring additional conditions to be met.

In order to prevent abuse the Act imposes several safeguards, including:

- Entrenchment will not prevent alteration where all of the members agree to an alteration, or where the court orders an alteration to be made.
- If a company wishes to entrench an article provision after the company has been formed, it can only do so with the agreement of all the members of the company.

Now read the key points from chapter 2 overleaf.

****

Key points from chapter 2

- The constitution of a company is commonly referred to as the Memorandum of the company.

- The Memorandum contains the key features of the company's status.

- Under the 2006 Companies Act the status of the Memorandum has been reduced and the Articles of Association is now the most important document.

- A company may change its name by special resolution in general meeting.

- The courts have long held that a companies articles form a contract between a company and its members, and between the members themselves

****

Chapter 3

Company Finance

The role and definition of the promoter

Although there is no statutory definition of a promoter, case law has developed as definition. In the case Twycross v Grant (1877) a promoter is defined as "one who undertakes to form a company with reference to a given project and to set it going, and who takes the necessary steps to accomplish that purpose."

In Emma silver Mining Co v Grant (1879) Lord Lindley stated that the term had no very definite meaning. Whether or not a person is a promoter is a question of fact. Promoters are quite often a company's first directors. The importance of establishing whether a person is a promoter lies partly in locating liability for acts done on behalf of or in connection with the company to be formed, for example, for statements in prospectuses. Not yet being in existence, the company cannot be liable. Promoters are not necessarily partners with each other (Keith Spicer and Mansell (1970)). Mainly it rests in deciding whether a person owes promoters fiduciary duty to the company.

Liability of a promoter

A promoter may become liable to third parties for misrepresentation or perhaps as the partner of another promoter under agency principles in partnership law. The traditional area of liability to the company is for breach of the fiduciary duties he owes it during his time of promotion.

Equity will not allow the promoter to taking advantage of his privileged position in relation to the unborn company. He must make full disclosure to it, when formed, of his interest in any transaction and must not profit from his position without the company's free consent. Otherwise, he must account personally for profits made and hold on constructive trust any property received which came to him by virtue of being a promoter.

A promoter must disclose fully the extent and the nature of his interest and profit. The duty cannot be avoided by setting up a company with a board of directors which cannot, and does not "exercise an independent and intelligent judgment on the transaction" and disclosing merely to that board.

In Erlanger v New Sombrero (1878) a syndicate headed by Erlanger, a French banker, acquired for £55,000 a lease of an island in the West Indies with phosphate mining rights. Erlanger then arranged for the syndicate to set up a company and to appoint its first directors, who were in reality puppets. The lease was sold, through a first party nominee, to the new company for £110,000 and within days of the company being established, the sale and purchase were ratified by the directors. The full details were not disclosed to members of the public who became shareholders. After the initial phosphate shipments proved unsuccessful, the true circumstances were revealed and the shareholders replaced the board of directors. It was held that the sale of the lease should be rescinded, the lease to be returned to the syndicate, which had to repay the purchase price to the company. The directors should not contribute to disadvantaging the shareholders. Disclosure to the members would be effective if they acquiesced (Lagunas Nitrate v Lagunas Syndicate (1899) but not if an undue advantage over investors remained e.g. if the original members comprised or were otherwise under the influence of the promoters (Gluckstein v Barnes) (1990).

Remedies

The company may be able to rescind contracts entered into consequent upon non-disclosure or misrepresentation by a promoter unless one of the bars to rescission has become operative i.e. affirmation (unless this amounts to ratification of breach of duty by way of fraud on the minority: Atwool v Merryweather (1867); lapse of time; intervening third party rights; inability to make restitutio in integrum; and the courts discretion to award damages in lieu of rescission (Misrepresentation Act 1967 s2 (2)).

Breach of fiduciary duty may result in liability to account and/or imposition of a constructive trust. But promoters should be able to retain expenses incurred in acquiring property in such cases (Bagnall v Carlton (1877)).

Remuneration and expenses

The promoter does his work and incurs expenses by the nature of his position, at a time before the company has become legally capable of acting. The company cannot therefore enter into a binding contract with him to pay him, nor can the company when formed validly ratify such an agreement made when it did not exist (retrospectively validate).

It cannot enter into a new contract after formation (except under seal) for the consideration he provides will be past.

The practical solution is for promoters to secure the insertion in the articles of a provision enabling the directors to pay promoter's expenses plus reasonable remuneration, which provision will be valid if full disclosure is made.

Pre-incorporation contracts

Similar difficulties arise with contracts purporting to be made between the company and third parties before incorporation. The company will not normally be bound by preliminary contracts. Nor will the promoter be liable for breach of implied warranty of authority if no implication can be made, the third party knowing the true facts. The company may be liable apart from contract, to pay a reasonable amount for benefits actually received, or for conversion, for refusing to permit the third party to retake goods delivered.

Rather than attempt to bind a company, a promoter might contract personally with a third party and forward benefits received to the company when formed, under a separate contract, subject to full disclosure. He might make the company liable on his original contract by assignment.

Under The Companies Act 2006 s 21:

"A contract that purports to be made by or on behalf of a company at a time when the company has not been formed, has effect, subject to any agreement to the contrary, as one made with the person purporting to act for the company or as an agent for it, and he is personally liable on the contract accordingly."

The company's agent will be personally liable whether he purports to act on behalf of the company or signs the contract in the company's name alone, and he may be personally liable as both parties know the company is about to be formed and is not yet at the stage of being formed (Phonogram v Lane (1981). However, a person carrying out the affairs of an existing company under a new name which has not yet been registered will not be personally liable. Such a company is not one which has not been formed (Oshkosh B'Gosh v Dan Marbel (1988).

Trading certificate

A public company initially registered as such cannot commence business until the registrar receives a declaration that the nominal value of the allotted share capital meets the authorised minimum and, satisfied that it is, issues a trading certificate, (Companies Act 2006). This provision can be avoided by registering as a private company and registering as a public one.

Rules relating to payment for shares

The following matters should be checked where shares are to be issued by a public or private company:

- Does the company have sufficient authorized share capital for the issue?

This may be checked by looking at the company's memorandum. If necessary, the authorized capital may be increased.

- Do the directors have authority to allot the shares? See s. 549 of the CA 2006. However, a private company may pass an elective resolution that s. 549 is not to apply to that company, since, normally, authority under s.551 of the CA 2006 can only last for a maximum period of five years, unless renewed.

- Do pre-emption rights apply? Section 561 of the CA 2006 makes statutory provision for pre-emption on second and subsequent issues of shares. This may be excluded by a private company in its constitution. It may be excluded by both private and public companies by special resolution.

The rules for payment for shares are based upon the Second EC Directive on company law. They are incorporated into the CA 2006. Section 582 (1) of the CA 2006 requires that shares should be paid up in money or money's worth. Section 582 (1) of the CA 2006 provides that a public company cannot accept an undertaking from a person to do work or perform services for shares.

Section 580 of the CA 2006 requires that shares cannot be issued at a discount. This applies to both public and private companies. There are, however, exceptions to this principle:

- Shares may be issued to underwriters at a discount of up to 10 per cent (s. 553 of the CA 2006)
- Shares may be issued in exchange for services that happen to be overvalued in a private company. Shares may not be issued in exchange for services in a public company.

- Shares may be issued in exchange for property which is overvalued in a private company. In a public company, there is a need for an independent expert valuation of the property concerned (s. 593 CA 2006).

In a public company shares must be paid up at least one quarter of their nominal value plus the whole of any premium (CA 2006 s 586)

A public company cannot issue shares in exchange for a non cash consideration which may be transferred more than five years from the date of allotment (s. 587 (1) CA 2006). Where shares are issued at a premium (that is above their nominal value) in either a public or private company, the whole of the premium is placed in a share premium account. This is treated as if it were ordinary share capital for most purposes. It cannot be used to pay up a dividend. However, it may be used to pay up a bonus issue of shares (s. 610 CA 2006).

Small Business, Enterprise and Employment Act 2015: abolition of bearer shares

The Small Business, Enterprise and Employment Act 2015 received Royal Assent at the end of the last Parliament. The fuller implications will be discussed in chapter 4. However, although the proposal is to stagger the implementation of most provisions over the next year, the changes to bearer shares come into force in May

2015. Affected companies and shareholders need to take immediate action.

The key provisions

From 26 May 2015, the issue of new share warrants to bearer (also known as bearer shares) will not be permitted. 26 May 2015 is the "commencement date" in a strict nine month timetable during which the holders of bearer shares will have the right to surrender the warrants for conversion into registered shares. Companies with bearer shares in issue must give various notices to the holders (including putting notices in the Gazette) informing them of their right to convert the bearer shares and the consequences of not doing so. The first notice must be given within the period of one month following the commencement date.

Companies will be obliged to apply to court to cancel bearer shares if they are not surrendered for conversion within the surrender period and pay into court the amount of share capital (nominal and premium) paid up on the bearer shares to be cancelled, plus any accrued dividends.

Implications

Although bearer shares are not often used in UK companies now, they have been used historically, for example, for structuring and tax planning. Companies should contact holders of bearer shares now so that the shares can be converted, avoiding the need to apply to court for the cancellation of unconverted bearer shares and having to fund the payment into court of the amount of share capital to be cancelled. Public companies with bearer shares should pay particular attention to the amount of share capital attributable to the bearer shares because any cancellation of bearer shares which results in the share capital dropping below the minimum required by the Companies Act 2006, may force the company to re-register as a private company.

There are criminal sanctions for both the company and its officers for default in complying with the provisions. Holders of warrants who do not surrender their bearer shares for conversion within the nine month surrender period will lose their shares. Monies paid into court can be claimed for up to three years following cancellation, but only where the failure to exercise the right of surrender was due to "exceptional circumstances". Unclaimed monies will go to the Government.

The supervision and control of investments

The Financial Services Act 1986, as amended by the Financial Services and Markets Act 2000, provides for a regime to protect investors. The Act provides statutory regulation and self-regulation by the market. Deposit taking businesses are regulated by the Banking Act 1987.

The Financial Services Act, as amended, gives certain functions to the Secretary of State but also authorises that person to transfer such functions as felt appropriate to a designated agency. This has been done in the first place to the Securities and Investment Board (S.I.B.) a body formed and supported mainly by the financial services industry. Those who carry on an investment business must be "authorised persons" of whom a register is kept (FSA 1986 s102) or "exempted persons". (FSA 1986 s3). Otherwise they commit an offence and all transactions are unenforceable.

Authorisation may be made by membership of a recognised professional body (FSA 1986 ss15-21) or by the Secretary of State (FSA 1986 s25). The commercial method is by membership of a recognised self-regulating organisation such as the Financial Intermediaries, Managers and Brokers Regulatory Association (FIMBRA). Exempted persons include: The Bank of England, clearing houses, Recognised Investment Exchanges such as the Stock Exchange and listed market institutions.

Except in the case of SRO's the Secretary of State is empowered to issue statements of principle and codes of practice regarding the conduct and financial standing expected of person authorised to carry on investment business (FSA 1986 ss57-58) and to make rules regulating the conduct of investment business by authorised persons for indemnification against civil liability incurred by authorised persons and for establishing a fund to compensate investors unable to obtain satisfaction of claims from authorised persons (FSA 1986 s54) and regulations with respect to money held by authorised persons (FSA 1986 s55).

The conduct of investment business

Subject to certain exceptions, the issue by or approval of an authorised person is necessary for the issue of an investment advertisment, which is an advertisement inviting people to enter into an investment agreement (FSA 1986 ss57-58). An investment agreement is one involving dealing or advising on investments, though not involving employee share schemes, sales of shares in private companies carrying over 75 percent of voting rights or where the terms of the transaction are uniform for all such transactions in the investment (FSA 1986 ss44(9) 20791) Sched 1). It is an offence knowingly or recklessly to make a misleading statement and to induce another to enter into, decline or refrain from exercising rights under an investment agreement, and without reasonably believing that he would not be so, to be involved in conduct creating a false impression as to the markets regarding investments and inducing a person to deal or refrain from dealing in those investments (FSA 1986 s 47).

On the Secretary of States application, the court may issue an injunction to prevent contravention of these provisions and order restitution of benefits (FSA 1986 s61).

The Securities market

For securities listed, or to be listed on the Stock Exchange it is necessary to comply with the requirements of the Financial Services Act 1986 part 1V. It empowers the Council of the Stock Exchange to make rules for this purpose, (FSA 1986 s142-144) including provisions for rectification for non-compliance with the rules. These rules on Admission of Securities to Listing (The Yellow Book) contain continuing disclosure requirements. Additionally to information required by the yellow book, the submitted listing particulars must contain such information as investors and their advisors would reasonably expect to make an informed assessment of the present and anticipated future rights and financial status of the securities (FSA 1986 ss146-148) and copies must be delivered to the registrar. Where listing particulars are to be published in connection with an application for listing, no other advertisement should be issued without the approval of the Stock Exchange (FSA 1896 s154).

A person acquiring relevant securities is entitled to be compensated by persons responsible for misleading particulars for loss suffered by reliance on the information unless they reasonably believed the statements or any detail were properly omitted (FSA 1986 ss150-152), but shareholders have no right to challenge cancellations of listing by judicial review (R v Stock Exchange ex p Else (1992).

Unlisted securities

Companies which are inadmissible to the Official Listed Market may apply for admission to the Alternative Investment Market (A.I.M.). Offers of unlisted securities are governed by FSA 1986 Part V (FSA 1986 s158).

A person may not be responsible for the issue of an advertisement offering securities to be admitted to an approved exchange (R.I.E.) without the approval of the exchange and the delivery to the Registrar (FSA 1986s 159) of a prospectus. Similarly, a prospectus must be registered if the person is responsible for the issue of an advertisement for securities which is a primary offer (i.e. one inviting the initial subscribing for or underwriting of securities) or a secondary offer (i.e. by a person who has acquired shares from a purchaser) though the Secretary of State can make an exemption in cases where the general public is unlikely to require the relevant information. Prospectuses must contain information prescribed by rules made by the Secretary of State and must contain all such information as investors and their professional advisors would reasonably expect to make an informed assessment of the present and anticipated rights and financial status of the securities (FSA 1986 ss163 and 164). Advertisements may not be issued for securities in private companies.

The main statutory rules are enhanced by the Public Offers of Securities Regulations 1995, which implement the E.C. Prospective Directive. They regulate first timer public offers of unlisted securities, subject to a number of exceptions (e.g. for denominations of less than ECU's 40,000). Free prospectuses must be published.

Subsequent dealings

A subsequent purchaser of securities on a market governed by the above rules should be protected by the securities having to comply with the rules governing the market. In addition, the ordinary law will also provide protection.

Criminal penalties and civil liability

The Financial Services Act, as amended, imposes a criminal liability for contravention of certain provisions. In addition it is an offence fraudulently or recklessly to induce someone to deposit money with any person (Banking Act 1987 s35). Under the Theft Act 1968 s19 a company officer causing or contributing to publication of a statement knowing it to be false or misleading, with intent to deceive members or creditors, may be imprisoned.

Civil liability

Whether on a first issue of or a subsequent dealing with shares, a person relying on a false statement may have a remedy against the company or the individual responsible. The following rules also apply:

- A person subscribing for or purchasing shares on the basis of misrepresentation may rescind the contract. The remedy is subject to the usual bars and to the courts discretion to award damages in lieu.

- Damages for breach of contract are unlikely to be available against the company, mainly because of the rules governing the maintenance of capital and equal rights of membership, but such damages might be claimed from a transferor of shares.

- A person intending to rely and actually relying on a false representation made knowingly or without belief in its truth or recklessly may sue for damages for deceit, but a purchaser of shares in the market cannot sue if the representation is made as an inducement only to original subscribers unless it is also meant to mislead subsequent purchasers or is reactivated by a later statement.

- A defendant issuing a prospectus may be liable for damages for negligence to a subsequent purchaser of the companies shares on the unlisted securities market if the defendant intended subsequent purchasers to rely on the prospectus.

- At least before liquidation begins, a person is now no longer debarred from obtaining compensation from a company simply by virtue of his status as a holder for applicant, or subscriber for, shares. The Financial Services Act 1986 entitles a person to receive compensation for loss caused by false listing particulars and prospectus without having to relinquish his membership.

- A person acquiring securities on the basis of a false statement in listing particulars or a prospectus may claim compensation from persons responsible subject to defences of reasonable belief, ignorance or disclaimer.
- Damages for breach of statutory duty might be recoverable for omission of statutorily required details from prospectuses and courts have a discretion to award compensation in criminal proceedings.

The raising and maintenance of capital-statement of capital

Companies can raise capital to finance activities in a number of ways. The deferral of payments, through the acquisition of items on hire purchase or lease terms is one way. For the raising of substantial sums a company will need to obtain loans at preferential rates and will, more often than not, issue debentures, a form of promise to pay at a fixed rate of interest. Debentures can be attractive, depending on interest rates and tax advantages. Debentures will be discussed in greater depth a little later.

Companies will issue shares to raise capital. This is another very common method of financing. Shares are split into different classes of preference share providing different returns and levels of security to appeal to different types of investor. The rights of any preference shareholder are limited to the terms of issue of the class of share allotted. A dividend may be paid following from which there is no entitlement to share in any further income. Shares may be redeemable (at any point) in which case the shareholder cannot vote at meetings. The class of share will determine the rights, obligations and ultimate gains of the shareholder.

Share capital can be nominal, in other words the amount of money the company's memorandum entitles the company to raise. This can comprise issued share capital and un-issued share capital. Paid up capital represents the money actually received from shares sold and uncalled capital the amount owed.

Reserve capital is uncalled capital which the company has resolved only to call up on liquidation (Companies Act 2006). Shares may be issued at a premium (for more than their nominal value) if so the extra value must be transferred to a share premium account. Profits undistributed as income are kept in a reserve fund.

The liability of members of limited companies is limited to the nominal value of their shares. The nominal value of a public company's share capital must not be less than the authorised minimum, currently £50,000 (Companies Act 2006). One quarter of the value of all issued shares of a public company plus any premiums must be paid up. Shares must not be issued at a discount although debentures may.

A commission may be paid to underwriters. Shares may be allotted for money or moneys worth. If shares are allotted for moneys worth, the consideration for allotment must be valued by an expert, whose report must be made to the company and made available to the allotee. Capital cannot be returned to members by the company. In general a company cannot acquire its own shares, subject to some exceptions (CA 2006 s 658).

A company must not provide financial assistance to another to acquire its or its holding company's shares. There are unconditional exceptions to this principle in s 681 of the CA 2006:

a) a distribution of the company's assets by way of a dividend lawfully made, or a distribution in the course of a company's winding up;

b) an allotment of bonus shares;

c) a reduction of capital'

d) a redemption of shares;

e) anything done in pursuance of an order of the court sanctioning compromise or arrangement with members or creditors;

f) anything done under an arrangement made in pursuance of s 110 of the Insolvency Act 1986;

g) anything done under an arrangement made between a company and its creditors that is binding on the creditors by virtue of Part 1 of the Insolvency Act 1986.

There are further exceptions for public companies in s 682 of the CA 2006:

- Companies may reduce their capital by passing a special resolution to this effect and obtaining the consent of the court to the reduction (s 641 (1) of the CA 2006)

- If a public company suffers a serious loss of capital (net assets worth half or less of called up share capital) then a general meeting is required to be called to alert the shareholders within 28 days of discovering that the loss of capital has occurred. The meeting should take place within 56 days (s 656 of the CA 2006).

Dividends to shareholders

Under s 820 the rules of the CA 2006 (from 2008) apply to 'every description of a company's assets to its members, whether in cash or otherwise'. Section 830 (2) of the CA 2006 provides that distributions can only Section 831 of the CA 2006 applies to public companies. It requires the public company to maintain the capital side of its account in addition to having available profits. Therefore, if the company's net assets are worth less than the subscribed share capital plus undistributable reserves at the end of the trading period, that shortfall must first be made good out of distributable profits before a dividend can be made. If a dividend is wrongly paid, a member may be liable to repay it under s 847 of the CA 2006.

Directors who are responsible for unlawful distributions can be held liable for breach of duty. If the directors have relied on auditors in recommending a dividend, then the auditors may be liable.

Changes made by the The Small Business, Enterprise and Employment Act 2015

From June 2016, the Statement of Capital will be simplified. The changes remove the requirement to show the amount paid up and unpaid on each share. Instead, director(s) now need to show the aggregate amount unpaid on the total number of shares. This figure is more useful for shareholders and creditors as it shows money which is still due to the company.

Currently, a statement of capital needs to be provided every year on the annual return. Instead, it can now simply be shown on the confirmation statement that there have been no changes for that year. Director(s) will only need to provide a full statement of capital where changes have been made during the year. This will avoid having to provide duplicate information to the registrar.

Becoming a shareholder

A person can become a shareholder by subscribing to a company, as per its memorandum or having shares transferred to him by an existing shareholder. Companies must keep a register of the class and extent of the company's shareholdings. A share is an item of property and usually freely transferable. It gives the holder an interest in the company measured by a sum of money and entitling him to the rights contained in the articles of association. The value of the shares is generally their market price although a large number whose votes confer more may have a greater value.

Shareholders would usually have equal rights but companies can issue various classes of shares depending on the articles of association. The nominal value of a share specifies the maximum liability of a member of a company. A share in a public company must be paid up by at least 25 percent but the company can make calls on the holder up to its unpaid value.

The articles may give the company a lien over the share for calls on the holder up to the unpaid value. They often empower it to forfeit the share for unpaid calls. A lien is an equitable charge on the share. It becomes effective on a specified event. Thus a different equitable interest of which the company has interest overrides a lien for debts due from the member (which it could set off against dividends) if the member only becomes indebted after the interest arose.

Under the Companies Act 2006, a company must, within two months of the allotment of shares or debentures or within two months of the lodging of a transfer of such securities, complete certificates, unless it is otherwise provided in their original issue, or it is not entitled to a certificate by virtue of the Stock Transfer Act 1982 (governing transfer of securities through a computerised system), or the allotment is to or the lodging of transfer is with a

Stock Exchange nominee, or it is excused under the Uncertificated Securities Regulations 1995.

Transfer and transmission of securities

Formal documentation is usually necessary for the transfer of shares. However, the Secretary of State has been authorised to provide by regulation for title to securities to be evidenced and transferred without a written instrument. Otherwise shares are freely transferable. Articles of association may restrict transfer in which case a refusal to register must be made within two months of its being lodged and must not be made in bad faith. The seller should transfer his share certificate to the buyer so that the company will readily consent to registering him as a member. If the seller only transfers part of his holding, he should deposit his share certificate with the stock exchange (if PLC) or the company, which will issue a certificate of transfer. Fully paid registered securities may be transferred by a stock transfer form approved under the Stock Transfer Act 1963. For a transfer to be registered by the company, unless the transfer is exempted by the Stock Transfer Act 1982, an instrument of transfer must be delivered to the company by either the transferor or the transferee.

Insider dealing

In recent years in particular, there has been controversy over the use of confidential information affecting the values of securities which is taken into account by the person in possession of it in deciding whether to buy or sell shares so as to make a profit. Insider trading, the use of knowledge by people on the inside of companies is seen as commercially immoral. However, it is extremely difficult to prevent. The only real deterrent is to impose criminal sanctions and to increase the powers of the various regulatory bodies. The Stock Exchange requires listed companies to adopt its Model Code for Securities Transactions for Directors and to secure compliance with it. The Code warns directors to avoid insider dealing and requires them to refrain from dealing within two months before announcement of the company's results and to notify the company of such dealings.

The common law position in relation to insider dealing is based on Percival v Wright (1902). Shareholders offered to sell shares to directors who knew their true value was greater because of an impending takeover bid, which information their confidential obligations to the company forbade them to disclose. For that reason it was decided that the shareholders could not rescind the contract. The directors had no general duty to the shareholders to disclose price sensitive information to them.

The Companies Act 2006 imposes a statuary prohibition by making it a criminal offence for a director to purchase an option to buy or sell quoted shares or debentures to a company in his group.

This liability is extended to his wife and children unless they had no reason to believe he was a director. The Companies Act also enacts requirements for disclosure and publicity. A director must disclose to the company details concerning the acquisition or disposal of any beneficial interest to himself, his wife or children in the group. If the shares are quoted the company must pass the information on to the stock exchange which may publish it. Any shareholders knowingly acquiring or disposing of a notifiable interest in voting shares (5 percent) in a public company must notify the company, which must keep a register of such interests.

There is also some administrative control.. Under the CA 2006, the Secretary of State can appoint inspectors to investigate suspected breaches of the various areas of the Companies Act.

The Financial Services Act 1986, as amended

There are certain provisions of the Financial Services Act that may apply to insider dealing. A private investor or other person suffering a loss from breach of a relevant rule may sue for damages for breach of statutory duty under the Financial Services Act ss61-62A.

The Criminal Justice Act 1993 Part V

If an individual knowingly has information which is insider information then he commits an offence if:

- Where the acquisition or disposal occurs on a regulated market, or where he acts or relies on a professional intermediary, he deals price affected securities.

- He encourages another person to deal in such securities knowing or having reasonable cause to believe that the acquisition or disposal occurs on a regulated market, or that the person dealing acts as or relies on a professional intermediary.

- He discloses the information to another person other than in the proper performance of his employment, office or profession.

The offence is punishable by a fine and/or up to seven years imprisonment. The Act has other provisions which provide for further sanctions and defences.

Borrowing money

In addition to issuing shares a company can raise finance by borrowing money. This is usually done in the longer term by issuing debentures. A Company may create a debenture fund and issue certificates for particular parts of the fund. The rights of debenture holders are fixed by the contract governing the loan. This is incapable of being altered even if, along the way, the articles are altered. Any attempted alterations represent a breach of contract.

Charges

Any form of security interest (fixed or floating) other than an interest arising by operation of law, is for the purposes of the Companies Act 2006 (Registration of charges) known as a charge.

Fixed and floating charges

A company can create a fixed charge over part of its property for the amount of the loan. Where a fixed charge is inappropriate, i.e. over fluctuating assets a floating charge over the whole or part of the company's assets can be made. The value of the charge as security depends on the assets in the company's possession at the time.

A charge must be registered within 21 days of its creation or the acquisition of property subject to it. The company and any officer at fault may be fined for non-registration. The court has discretion to extend a registration period. The Companies Act 2006 lists the registrable charges, including those on land, goods, intangible moveable property, i.e. intellectual property, for securing issues of debentures and floating charges. Not every charge is registrable, this very much depends on the nature of the charge.

Effects of non-registration

Where a registrable charge created by the company is not registered, the security is void against an administrator or liquidator of the company and any person who for value acquires an interest in or right over property subject to the charge where the beginning of insolvency proceedings, or acquisition occurs after the charge's creation. Where the registered particulars are not complete or accurate the charge is void, unless a court orders otherwise.

A registered charge, in general, gives the chargee a prior right, according to its terms, over a subsequent charge and any previous unregistered charges. But a subsequent floating charge can be created over a particular part of the assets covered by a previous floating charge over the wider category. A later fixed charge will gain priority over a previous floating charge covering the assets in question. In either case this is because floating charges are created with knowledge of the possibility of subsequent dealings with assets.

Unregistered chargees may prove in a company's liquidation as unsecured creditors and rank in priority as such. Fixed chargees can simply enforce their security according to the terms of the charge. The rights of floating chargees are, however, postponed to those entitled to preferential payments on a winding up (s196).

A floating charge created within 12 months of the onset of insolvency (24 months if in favour of a person connected with the company) or between the presentation of a petition for and the consequent making of an administration order is, unless the charge is not connected with the company and the company was solvent immediately after its creation, void except to the amount of any consideration provided simultaneously with or subsequent to its creation, plus interest.

Now read the key points from chapter 3 overleaf.

Key points from chapter 3

- A promoter is defined as "one who undertakes to form a company with reference to a given project and to set it going, and who takes the necessary steps to accomplish that purpose".

- A public company initially registered as such cannot commence business until the registrar receives a declaration that the nominal value of the allotted shares meets the authorized minimum.

- Companies can issue shares in a variety of ways.

- The Financial Services Act 1986 provides for a regime to protect investors.

- Companies which are inadmissible to the Official Listed market may apply for admission to the Alternative Investment Market (AIM).

- Companies can raise capital to finance activities in a number of ways. Loans and debentures are two typical ways.

- The liability of members of a limited company is limited to the value of their shares.

- Shareholders will receive dividends when a company is trading profitably. There are different types and classes of shareholder.

- The The Small Business, Enterprise and Employment Act 2015
- In recent years. insider trading has become more prevalent. This is a criminal offence.

Chapter 4

Company Management

The duties of a director

Director's duties can be split into two parts – the director's duty of care and skill and the director's fiduciary duties. The rules governing directors duties are now codified in the CA 2006 s171-177.

The CA 2006 provides that:

- The matters to which the directors of a company are to have regard in the performance of their functions include the interests of the company employees in general as well as the interests of the members.

- Accordingly, the duties of this section imposed on the directors of a company is owed by them to the company (and the company alone) and is enforceable in the same way as any other fiduciary duty owed to a company by its directors.

Section 247 of the Companies Act 2006 permits a company to make payments to its employees on ceasing to trade or on transferring the business. Previously, this had been ultra vires where there was no business that was capable of being benefited.

The duty of care and skill

The duty of care and skill, owed to a company by its directors has traditionally been interpreted in such a way that places a very modest burden on the shoulders of its directors. However, under the CA 2006 the general duties of directors has been placed on a statutory basis. This can be found in s 170 of the CA 2006. Section 170 (3) states that:

....the general duties are based on certain common law rules and equitable principles as they apply in relation to directors and have effect in place of those rules and principles as regards the duties owed to a company by a director.

s. 170 (4) of the CA 2006 states that

The general rules shall be interpreted and applied in the same way as common law rules or equitable principles, and regard shall be had to the corresponding common law rules and equitable principles in interpreting and applying the general duties.

The leading case is Re City Equitable Fire and Insurance Co Ltd (1925). In this case there had been a serious shortfall of funds and the managing director was convicted of fraud. The liquidator also wanted to implicate three other directors in the fraud. The judge in the case, Romer J set out three basic propositions which constituted the duties of directors:

" A director need not exhibit in the performance of his duties a greater degree of skill than may reasonably be expected from a person of his knowledge and experience. A director of a life insurance company, for instance, does not guarantee that he has the skill of an actuary or a physician. In the words of Lord Lindley, MR, " If the directors act within their powers, if they act with such care as is reasonably to be expected from them having regard to their knowledge and experience, and if they act honestly for the benefit of the company they represent, they discharge both their equitable and their legal duty to the company" (Lagunas Nitrate Co v Lagunas Syndicate (1899).

Although the above statement, summing up director's duties, puts forward the notion of a somewhat limited duty of care there are indications that the nature of care and skill is changing somewhat. Section 214 of the Insolvency Act 1986 provides for an objective standard of care in relation to directors and shadow directors where the company is insolvent and they ought to have recognised that fact. In Norman v Theodore Goddard (1991) Hoffman J accepted that the standard applied in s214 applied generally in relation to directors. The second proposition put forward by Romer J in Re City Equitable relates to the attention that has to be paid to the affairs of the company and states:

"

A director is not bound to give continuous attention to the affairs of a company. His duties are of an intermittent nature to be performed at periodic board meetings and meetings of any committees of the board upon which he happens to be placed. He is not, however, bound to attend all such meetings, though he ought to attend whenever, in the circumstances, he is reasonably able to do so."

The third proposition set out by Romer J is as follows:

" In respect of all duties that, having regard to all the exigencies of business and the articles of association, may properly be left to some official, a director is, in the absence of grounds for suspicion, justified in trusting that official to perform such duties honestly."

Fiduciary duties

The term "fiduciary duties" describes the other duties owed by directors to their company. Both statute and case law heavily govern this area. While, as seen above, there is little expectation of a director in relation to care and skill, there is great expectation in relation to honesty and integrity.

The Companies Act 2006 s 182 (1) requires directors to make disclosures. There is a requirement for a director to disclose any interest that he has between himself and the company. The provision also covers connected persons, such as family, another company with which the director is associated controlling more than 20 percent of the voting capital, a trustee of a trust whose beneficiaries include the director himself or a connected person, a partner of a director or of a connected person. The Companies Act 2006 further elaborates. A shadow director is also required to comply with The CA 2006 s 182 as well as a director. Disclosure should be to the full board. Mere compliance with the section does not entitle a director to keep any profits. In order to keep any profits, the director must be able to rely on a provision in the company's constitution or have his retention of the profit ratified by the company in general meeting.

Some contracts require prior authorisation by the company in general meeting. Section 190 (1) of the Companies Act 2006 applies to what are termed substantial property transactions. If the director or a shadow director is to sell or purchase from the company one or more no-cash assets that are substantial, then prior approval in general meeting is needed. A transaction is substantial if the market value of the asset exceeds the lower of £100,000 or 10 percent of the company's net asset value.

Transactions worth less than £2,000 are never substantial. Section 190 (1) also applies to connected persons.

Section 323 prohibits a director or shadow director of a company from buying options on shares or debentures of the company or its holding company or its subsidiaries. The penalty for infringement is a fine or imprisonment. The Companies act 2006 requires a director or shadow director to notify the company of any interest in the shares or debentures of the company or subsidiaries.

A director must not place himself in a position where his interests conflict with the company's interests. The leading case here is Regal (Hastings) v Gulliver 1942. Regal owned a cinema in the town of Hastings and wished to acquire two other cinemas in the area, at the suggestion of the company solicitor. The company did not have funds for the purchase and it was suggested that the solicitor, the directors and the company itself should put up the money. This was successful, improving the finances of the company. The company was sold as a going concern, to a purchaser who bought the company's shares. The company, under new management then began an action against the erstwhile directors for damages in respect of the profit that they had made on the sale of their shares. It was established that the directors had acted from prudent financial motives and there was no damages due. The House of Lords thought different and held that the directors had acquired the shares in exploitation of their position as directors. They had not obtained the consent of the company and had to reimburse the company.

The same principle has been established in later decisions. However, not every case of a director taking an opportunity that has come by way of the company will be committing a breach of duty. If the company has turned down the opportunity without any proper influence from the director and the director takes it up subsequently, there is no reason why the director cannot retain the profit. A number of high profile cases have borne this out, for example, Peso Silver Mines v Cropper, (1966) and Island Export Finance Limited v Umunna (1986).

A related area is the question of competition. To what degree is the director of a company able to compete with the company of which he is a director, either through another company or a partnership or trading as a sole trader. The case of London and Mashonaland Exploration Co Ltd v New Mashonaland Exploration Co Ltd (1891) has found that it does not involve a breach of duty. However, in spite of the above case, the position of a director competing against his company is untenable. If a director is director of two companies in this situation then clearly he would be in breach of duty to one or another company.

There are areas of law which indicate that competition is not permissible. In Hivac Ltd v Park Royal Scientific Instruments Ltd (1946) senior employees engaged on sensitive work in wartime were not able to compete with their employer. However, the fact that it was wartime makes this decision rather special. Thus, director's powers must be exercised in a fiduciary way. The overall duty is one of trust, which must be borne out by integrity.

Directors personal liability

Directors may be liable in contract for:

- Breach of warranty of authority.
- A collateral guarantee.
- Pre–incorporation contracts under The Companies Act 2006.

Tort

Directors may be liable in tort:

- For fraud in relation to listing particulars and prospectuses.
- For negligent misstatement in relation to listing particulars and prospectuses.
- For a breach of personal duty and care.

Statute

Directors may be liable under statute:

- For misstatements or omissions in listing particulars (s.150 of the Financial Services Act 1986).
- For improper use of the company name (The Companies Act 2006).

Directors may be liable under other legislative provisions including:

- Section 213 of the Insolvency Act 1986 in relation to fraudulent trading.
- Section 214 of the Insolvency Act 1986 in relation to wrongful trading.
- Section 216 of the Insolvency Act 1986 in relation to Phoenix Companies under prohibited names.
- Under other legislation particularly health and safety and the environment, such as the Health and Safety at Work Act 1974, the Control of Pollution Act 1974 and the Water Industry Act 1991.

Limiting liability of directors

The Companies Act 2006 prohibits the exclusion of directors from liability but makes it possible to provide insurance for directors. The Companies Act 2006 allows courts to relieve directors of liability if thought that they have acted reasonably and honestly.

The role of the company secretary

The Company secretary is one of the principal officers of the public company. As stated there is now no requirement for a private company to have a secretary. The company secretary is the agent through whom most of the company's administrative work is done.

The following are some of the company secretary's responsibilities:

- Preparation and keeping of minutes (s248 CA 2006)
- Dealing with share transfers and issuing share and debenture certificates
- Keeping and maintaining the register of members and debenture holders s113 (1) and 743 (6) of the CA 2006..
- Keeping and maintaining the registers of directors and secretary s 804 2006 CA.
- The registration of charges and maintaining the company's register of charges. S 860 to 876 CA 2006.
- Keeping and maintaining the register of directors share interests s 809 2006 CA.
- Keeping the records of the director's service contracts s 328 CA
- The collation of directors interests that have to be disclosed.
- Keeping and maintaining the register of material share interests. S 808 (1) CA 2006
- Sending notices of meetings, copies of accounts etc.
- Keeping the company's constitution up to date.
- Preparation and submission of the annual return.
- Filing of returns and documents.
- Preparation of returns required by government departments.
- Witnessing documents together with a director.
- Payment of dividends and the preparation of dividend warrants.

These are most of the duties but there are other matters, such as employment issues, which may become the responsibility of the company secretary. In a Public Limited Company the Companies Act 2006 requires the secretary to hold a recognised professional qualification before taking up such a post.

The role of company auditors

Every company must appoint auditors, except dormant companies and private companies which are exempt from the audit requirements (Companies Act 2006). An auditor may be removed by ordinary resolution of the company. Special notice must be served and the auditor can make representation and seek compensation.

An auditor may resign from office under the Companies Act 2006, circulating a statement as to why and setting out any irregularities which he thinks should be brought to the attention of the board. When an auditor does deposit a statement of circumstances, which he wishes to bring to the attention of members or creditors, he may deposit a requisition with the statement requiring the company to call an extraordinary general meeting. The auditor who is removed or who has resigned may attend the meeting to appoint new auditors. The auditors have a duty to audit company accounts (s485-520 of the Companies Act 2006). The auditor has to be particularly rigorous. The duties of an auditor have been outlined by Lord Denning:

- First the auditors should verify the arithmetical accuracy of the accounts and the proper vouching entries in the books.

- Secondly, the author should make checks to test whether the accounts mask errors or even dishonesty.

- Thirdly, the auditor should report on whether the accounts give to the shareholders reliable information respecting the true financial position of the company (Lord Denning in Foment (Sterling Area Ltd v Selsden Fountain Pen Company Limited (1958)

Auditors liabilities

An auditor is required to investigate suspicious circumstances. In Re Thomas Gerrard (1967) it was noted that:

"The standards of reasonable care and skill are from the expert evidence more exacting than those which prevailed in 1896" (Re Kingston Cotton Mill).

In this case, in addition to an overstatement of stock, there had been fraudulent practice in changing invoice dates to make it appear that client's owed money within the accounting period when, in fact, it was due outside of it, and to make it appear that suppliers were not yet owed money for goods when such liability did exist. The auditors in this case were held liable. Liability may arise in contract. The auditor will be liable for failing to perform properly what he has undertaken to do. The other party to the contract – the company – is the only person who can sue the company under this head of liability.

An auditor may be liable in negligence to his client or in the tort of negligent misstatement to third parties. An auditor may also be liable for a winding up for misfeasance or breach of duty to the company (section 212 of the Insolvency Act 1986). Where this has occurred the court will order compensation as it thinks appropriate.

The Small Business, Enterprise and Employment Act 2015
The Small Business, Enterprise and Employment Act received Royal Assent in March 2015. Significant changes have been made to the adminsitartion of companies in particular the maintenance of records. Outlined below are the main changes, although not in date order.

People with significant control (PSC) register
Companies, LLPs and SEs need to keep a register of people with significant control ('PSC register') from 6 April 2016. A PSC is anyone in a company, LLP or SE who meets one or more of the conditions listed in the legislation.

This is someone who:

- owns more than 25% of the company's shares
- holds more than 25% of the company's voting rights
- holds the right to appoint or remove the majority of directors
- has the right to, or actually exercises significant influence or control
- holds the right to exercise or actually exercises significant control over a trust or company that meets one of the first 4 conditions.

Protecting PSC information -

From 6 April 2016 The PSC's usual residential address won't be available on the public register, and the day of birth will be suppressed. All other PSC information will be available on the public register, much like directors and members details are currently held. In some exceptional cases, it may be that a PSC is at risk of violence or intimidation. For example, this might be because they're linked to a company that might be targeted by activists due to its activities. In these cases, directors may apply to have their details protected, so they aren't available to credit reference agencies. If protection is granted the directors still need to send PSC information to companies house when it's required (for example on the confirmation statement), and the information will still be available to the police.

Filing PSC information

From 30 June 2016 companies are already keeping a 'PSC register' by this point. This information now needs to be filed with companies house on incorporation and updated when directors submit later 'confirmation statements'. It's a criminal offence to not provide this information.

Confirmation statement - June 2016

From 30 June 2016, the annual return has been replaced. Instead, directors now file a confirmation statement at least once a year. They need to check and confirm the company information that is held for the company and let companies house know if there are any changes. To complete the confirmation statement a director needs to:

- check the information held on the registered office, directors and location of registers – if there's been any changes, there is the need to complete a separate form before filing the confirmation statement
- check and if necessary update the shareholder information, statement of capital and the standard industry classification (SIC code)
- check and confirm the record is up to date
- pay the £13 fee to file online or £40 by paper (2017)

The due date for the confirmation statement is usually a year after the incorporation of the company or the date directors filed the last annual return.

Statement of capital – from June 2016

As stated in the previous chapter dealing with shareholders, statement of capital will be simplified. The changes remove the requirement to show the amount paid up and unpaid on each share. Instead, directors now need to show the aggregate amount unpaid on the total number of shares. This figure is more useful for shareholders and creditors as it shows money which is still due to the company. Currently, a statement of capital needs to be provided every year on the annual return. Instead, directors can now simply show on the confirmation statement that there have been no changes for that year. Directors will only need to provide a full statement of capital where changes have been made during the year. This will avoid having to provide duplicate information to the registrar.

Accelerated strike-off – from 10 October 2015

The time it takes to strike a company off the register if it's not carrying on business or operation has been reduced. The accelerated strike-off process aims for the right balance between removing a defunct company from the register and allowing creditors time to register an objection. Under old legislation, if no objection was received, the company was struck off not less than 3 months after publication of a notice in The Gazette. Under the new timescales, the company is struck off not less than 2 months from publication of the Gazette notice.

Date of birth -from 10 October 2015

It's always been a requirement of the Companies Act 2006 for directors to provide a full date of birth. Companies House is now giving more protection by suppressing the day of birth on the public record. The full date of birth still needs to be provided to Companies House, but won't be shown in full on their data products or on images or new filings. The full date of birth will only be disclosed in exceptional circumstances (for example to credit reference agencies, or to the police). This procedure is similar to how residential addresses are protected.

Consent to act as an officer -from 10 October 2015

For newly appointed officers, companies house has added a statement to the relevant appointment and incorporation forms (paper and electronic) that the person has consented to act in their relevant capacity. Companies are required to agree to this statement. This replaced the previous consent to act procedure of providing a signature on paper forms and personal authentication on electronic filings.

As part of this, Companies House will write to all newly appointed directors to make them aware that their appointment has been filed on the public register and explain their general legal duties. See also the new director disputes procedure.

Director disputes -from April 2016

This measure provides a simpler way to get falsely appointed directors' details removed from the register. If an appointed director didn't consent to act in their appointment, they can apply to have the notification of their appointment removed from the register. When an application is received, the company in question will be asked to provide evidence the director 'consented to act' in their appointment. If sufficient evidence isn't provided, this will result in the director's appointment being removed from the register. This proof might be that the company has retained a statement from the director that they have 'consented to act'.

Registered office address (ROA) disputes - from April 2016

This will help when a company is using an address for its registered office without authorisation. Where a complaint is received that a company or a limited liability partnership (LLP) is wrongly using an ROA, Companies House will investigate. If the registrar is satisfied that a company or LLP is not entitled to use an address, they'll be able to change the ROA of that company or LLP to the 'default' address.

Default addresses

The registrar can nominate a default address for each jurisdiction (England and Wales, Scotland or Northern Ireland). Any post sent to a company at the default address will be held at the relevant Companies House office. Companies House offices won't receive packages or bailiff visits for companies whose ROA has been changed to a default address.

Evidence of ROA

Acceptable evidence that a company has the right to use an ROA might be a document that shows it's a building the company owns, one they rent, or an agreement from the owner that they are allowed to use the address as an ROA. The registrar will consider any evidence sent and advise both the company and the applicant of the outcome. If the registrar can't come to an appropriate decision, it may be referred to the courts.

Company registers – from June 2016

Private companies will be able to opt to keep certain information on the public register, instead of holding their own statutory registers. This will apply to registers of:

- members
- directors
- secretaries
- directors' residential addresses
- people with significant control (PSC)

This is voluntary, and a company can continue holding its own registers if preferred.

Directors misconduct - from October 2015

From October 2015, new offences were added to the current regime that individuals can also be disqualified for.

These are:

- 'disqualification for certain convictions abroad'
- 'disqualification of persons instructing unfit directors'

The conduct of people instructing unfit directors can also be taken into consideration. If a director has been deemed unfit due to someone exercising control over the director, they could also be –

Bearer Shares-from 26 May 2015

Share warrants to bearer (known as 'bearer shares') were abolished. These were shares issued by a company, but assigned to a warrant, rather than a registered owner. The warrant allowed the bearer holder to claim any ownership or rights attached to those shares. As the owner's details did not need to be entered into the register of members, it was sometimes difficult to establish ownership of those shares. All shares must now have a designated owner.

If a company has bearer shares

If this affects a company, the bearer shareholders have 9 months (from 26 May 2015) to surrender their warrants voluntarily. These can then be converted into registered shares, and the bearer shareholder will enter their name into the register of members. A company should take steps to ensure bearer shareholders know their rights to surrender their warrants, and the consequences if they don't.

Consequences of not surrendering share warrants

If the share warrants haven't been surrendered within 7 months (from 26 May 2015), all rights are automatically suspended. Bearer shareholders can't vote or claim dividends from the shares. They will also be unable to transfer the warrant, as any transfers made after the 7 month period are void. If the share warrants haven't been surrendered within 9 months, the company has to make an application to the court to have them cancelled.

Corporate directors

A company won't be able to appoint corporate directors, although there are some limited exceptions. The detail of these exceptions are still under development. Any further information including a date for implementation will be provided on GOV.UK as soon as it's available.

Now read the key points from Chapter 4 overleaf.

****

Key points from chapter 4

- Director's duties can be split into two parts: the director's duty of care and the directors fiduciary duties.

- A director must not place himself in a position where his interests conflict with the company's interests.

- Directors can be liable for negligence.

- The company secretary is one of the principal officers of the company with a wide range of responsibilities.

- There is no legal requirement for a private company to have a secretary.

- Every company must appoint auditors, except dormant companies and private companies.

- The Small Business, Enterprise and Employment Act 2015 has made significant changes to the way companies are adminstered.

****

Chapter 5

Company Meetings and Shareholder Protection

Company meetings

Decisions concerning the company's activities and also its future are decided in general meetings of the shareholders. The main law on this is in the Companies Act 2006, Part 13, Resolutions and Meetings (sec281 to sec361), particularly Chapter 3, Resolutions at meetings.

Usually decisions will be made at the Annual General Meeting of Shareholders, which must be held once every year for public companies for declaring dividends, considering accounts and the respective reports of directors and auditors, and for electing auditors and directors. S 336 of the CA 2006 abolishes the need for private companies to hold AGM's. Private companies may use written resolutions instead.

Section 303 of the CA 2006 allows two or more members holding 10% or more of the shareholding to require the calling of an Extraordinary General Meeting. Extraordinary general meetings can be called as and when the need arises and meetings of a particular class of members or creditors are called class meetings.

Resolutions

The law relating to resolutions has been changed by the Companies Act 2006. Private companies can pass resolutions either via written resolution (s 281 91)(a) of the CA 2006 or at a members meeting (s 281(1)(b) of the CA 2006. Under s 282 of the CA 2006 written resolutions can now be passed by a simple majority.

Special resolution

This is one passed by a majority of at least 75% of those voting after 21 days notice (s 283 CA 2006), eg a resolution to change the company's articles of association.

Ordinary resolution

This is defined in s 282 of the CA 2006 as a resolution passed by a simple majority of those voting. It will usually involve 14 days notice. On occasion, the courts have been willing to apply the 'assent principle' to unanimity where there has been no meeting regardless of the type of company involved.

Elective resolution

These have been abolished by the CA 2006.

Unanimous informal consent

Where there has been no formal resolution passed at a general meeting, if it can be shown that all the shareholders with the right to attend and vote at a general meeting have assented to some matter at a meeting, or not, which is within the powers of the general meeting to carry into effect, such assent is binding as a resolution passed in a properly convened general meeting (Re Duomatic Ltd (1969).

This principle has been applied in cases where there was a technical requirement for the general meeting to waive failures to comply with formalities (Re Express Engineering Works Ltd (1920) and cases involving an approval of directors remuneration (Re Duomatic Ltd (1969). However, the principle can only be applied to matters that are *ultra vires* to the company.

Votes

The Companies Act 2006 sets out a minimum standard for the conduct of votes in s 321. Votes are conducted first on a show of hands with one vote per member, proxies not voting unless the articles so provide. A poll may be demanded by any five members (here proxies count) or 10 per cent of the voting rights. A decision on a poll will override a decision on a show of hands.

Adjournment

At common law, there is a power to adjourn if there is disorder or if there is a problem accommodating all those turning up.

Minutes

Companies must keep minutes of all general meetings (s 248 of the CA 2006).

Majority rule in meetings

Company decisions are taken by its members, by majority vote. However, the members generally devolve the decision making to a board of directors. This devolution of power is achieved by majority vote. Majority is generally determined by the number of shares held and not by the number of shareholders.

Protection of minorities

There are two areas which need to be examined in relation to minority protection, the rule in the classic case of Foss v Harbottle (1843) and also statutory protection. The decision in Foss v Harbottle was connected to the acquisition of land in Manchester by a group of businessmen to be dedicated to Queen Victoria. Some of the members of the company alleged that certain directors had misapplied company property. It was alleged that the directors had taken for themselves a price exceeding the true value of the land. It was held that the action could not proceed, the wrong had not been done to individual shareholders but to the company. The judge stated:

"The Victoria Park Company is an incorporated body and the conduct with which the defendants are charged in this suit is an injury not to the plaintiffs exclusively, it is an injury to the whole corporation by individuals whom the corporation entrusted with powers to be exercised only for the good of the corporation."

The principle is that a company may ratify what it has done and that makes litigation pointless. There are exceptions to the principle established in this case which indicate that the majority cannot go unchecked:

- An ultra vires act, which by their nature could not be ratified by the majority.
- Minority shareholders can complain of a fraud on the minority.
- A bare majority cannot do something needing a larger majority.
- Individual members can always assert their individual rights.

The statutory remedy

Of far more importance in practice to the rule in Foss v Harbottle and its exceptions is the statutory remedy. The difficulties with Foss and Harbottle led to the introduction of a statutory remedy in s210 of the Companies Act 1948, then amended by section 75 of the Companies Act 1980, subsequently amended by the Companies Act 2006, which reads:

A member of a company may apply to the court by petition for an order under this part on the ground that the company's affairs are being or have been conducted in a manner which is unfairly prejudicial to the interests of its members generally or some part of its members (including at least himself) or that any actual or proposed act or omission of the company (including an act or omission on its behalf) is or would be so prejudicial.

The court has the power to award relief as it sees fit. It may make an order regulating the company's affairs or restrict the company from acting in a certain way.

One remedy available to the member is that of just and equitable winding up of a company. This may seem extreme in many cases. However, it is a powerful remedy open to the member. A company may be wound up by the court if the court is of the opinion that it is just and equitable that the company should be wound up (s 22(1)(g) of the Insolvency Act 1986).

The key case in relation to just and equitable winding up is Ebrahimi v Westbourne Galleries Ltd (1973). The House of Lords stated that the categories of conduct justifying winding up on the just and equitable ground are not closed. In Ebrahimi v Westbourne Galleries Ltd the ground was exclusion from management in a quasi partnership company. However, another ground on which just and equitable winding up may be awarded is if the purpose for which the company may be formed can no longer be achieved. This was the ground in Re German Date Coffee Co (1882). The company had been formed to obtain a German patent to manufacture coffee from dates. The application for the patent was refused. A petition to wind up the company was granted.

If there is a deadlock within a company and the deadlock cannot be solved then a petition to wind up a company will be successful. In Re Yenidje Tobacco Co Ltd (1916) the company had two shareholders with an equal number of shares. They were each directors. They could not reach agreement on how the company should be run. There was no provision for breaking the deadlock and a petition to wind the company up on the just and equitable ground was successful. One further ground for just and equitable winding up is that of dishonesty of directors.

Now read the key points from chapter 5 overleaf.

****

Key points from chapter 5.

- Decisions concerning the company's activities and also its future are decided in general meetings of the shareholders.

- Decisions in meetings are made by resolution.

- The articles of association will determine the necessary period of notice for meetings.

- The company has a duty to keep minutes of the meetings.

****

Chapter 6

Company Takeover and Mergers

A takeover of a company means the process by which one company gains control of another. Control means the ability to influence policy and control the board of directors, usually requiring more than 50 percent of the voting shares.

Private companies often have a provision in the articles of association allowing directors to refuse to register a transfer of shares, so that takeover will not be possible without the authority and consent of the directors.

Public companies, however, are very different. Public companies can offer shares to the public and are usually listed on the Stock Exchange. They often have large and very dispersed shareholdings. The usual procedure is for the offeror to send a circular to the shareholders in the target company making an offer to buy their shares. This circular is an 'investment invitation' and was subject to s57 of the Financial Services Act 1986 which has now been superseded by the Financial Services and Markets Act 2000.

Buyout and sellout

Rights

There are very few company laws governing takeovers, but the rights of offerors, when the majority of shareholders have accepted a bid, to acquire remaining shareholdings and of minority shareholders to require their shares to be bought are governed by The Companies Act 2006

Compulsory acquisition

The Companies Act provides a procedure to enable a takeover bidder who has acquired 90 percent of the shares in a company to acquire the remaining shares compulsorily. 90 percent means 90 percent of the shares that are subject to offer-this excludes shares that are already held by the offeror or associates. The terms must be the same as other shares bid for and the acquisition of 90 percent must be within 4 months of the offer being made. If 90 percent cannot be reached because some shareholders cannot be traced, but would otherwise be reached, then the court may authorise compulsory acquisition if it considers it to be just and equitable.

Intervention by the court

A shareholder can apply to the court within six weeks of the offer being made. The court can:

- Order that the offeror is not entitled to acquire the shares.
- Specify terms different from the offer.

Grounds for court intervention

The main ground is that the offer is unfair, despite the fact that 90 percent have accepted it (see Sussex Brick Company (1961)).

Requisition by shareholders to buy shares

A procedure is provided to enable a small minority of shareholders whose shares have not been bought in the takeover to require the offeror to buy them out.

The regulations are as follows:

- 90 percent time limit applies as for compulsory acquisition.
- The offeror must issue a compulsory acquisition notice or notify every shareholder who has not accepted offer of the right to be bought out.
- The requisition to the buyout must be in writing.
- Terms must be the same as for all other share bids for, or agreed by parties, or fixed by the court.
- There is a time limit which is the end of the period by which the offer can be accepted.

Self-regulation: The Panel on Takeovers and Mergers

The Panel on Takeovers and Mergers (the "Panel") is an independent body, established in 1968, whose main functions are to issue and administer the City Code on Takeovers and Mergers (the "Code") and to supervise and regulate takeovers and other matters to which the Code applies in accordance with the rules set out in the Code. It has been designated as the supervisory authority to carry out certain regulatory functions in relation to takeovers pursuant to the Directive on Takeover Bids (2004/25/EC) (the "Directive"). Its statutory functions are set out in and under Chapter 1 of Part 28 of the Companies Act 2006. The rules set out in the Code also have a statutory basis in relation to the Isle of Man, Jersey and Guernsey.

The Panel regulates takeover bids and other merger transactions (however effected) for companies which have their registered offices in the United Kingdom, the Channel Islands or the Isle of Man if any of their securities are admitted to trading on a regulated market or multilateral trading facility in the United Kingdom or on any stock exchange in the Channel Islands or the Isle of Man. Its remit also extends to other public companies and certain private companies which are resident in the United Kingdom, the Channel Islands or the Isle of Man. In certain circumstances the Panel also shares responsibility for the regulation of an offer with the takeover regulator in another Member State of the European Economic Area (a "Member State") (for example, where the offeree company is registered in the United Kingdom and has its securities admitted to trading on a regulated market in another Member State but not on a regulated market in the United Kingdom). Full details of the scope of the Panel's jurisdiction and of its responsibilities in shared jurisdiction cases are set out in section 3 of the Introduction to the Code.

The Code is designed to ensure that shareholders are treated fairly and are not denied an opportunity to decide on the merits of a takeover and that shareholders of the same class are afforded equivalent treatment by an offeror. The Code also provides an orderly framework within which takeovers are conducted. In addition, it is designed to promote, in conjunction with other regulatory regimes, the integrity of the financial markets. The Code is not concerned with the financial or commercial advantages or disadvantages of a takeover. These are matters for the company and its shareholders.

Wider questions of public interest, such as competition policy, are the responsibility of government and other bodies, such as the Competition Commission, the Office of Fair Trading and the European Commission.

Judicial review and the role of the court
It has been held that the Panel is subject to judicial review (R v Panel on Takeovers and Mergers ex parte Datafin (1987); R v Panel on

Takeovers and Mergers ex parte Guiness plc (1990)). The court recognises that the Panel is required to make decisions quickly and may give a ruling for future guidance rather than reverse a past decision.

Enforcement

The Code does not have the force of law, but works on the premise that 'those who seek to take advantage of the facilities of the securities markets in the United Kingdom should conduct themselves in matters relating to takeovers in accordance with best business standards and so according to the Code'.

The Code and Directors
Duties

Directors owe fiduciary duties to the company. In addition, General Principle 9 of the Code stipulates:

- Directors of an offeror and offeree company must always, in advising their shareholders, act only in their capacity as directors and not have regard to their personal or family shareholdings.
- Directors of the offeree company should give careful consideration before they enter into any commitment with an offeror which would restrict their freedom to advise their shareholders in the future.

- Such commitments may give rise to conflicts of interest or result in a breach of the directors fiduciary duties.

- It has been established that although directors owe a duty to shareholders to ensure that any information and advice is given in good faith and is not misleading, fiduciary duties are owed to the company (Dawson International plc v Coats Patons plc (1988)).

Now read the key points from chapter six overleaf

****

Key points from Chapter Six

- A takeover of a company means the process by which one company gains control of another

- The Companies Act 2006 provides a procedure to enable a takeover bidder who has acquired 90% of the shares in a company to acquire the remaining shares compulsorily

- A procedure is provided to enable a small minority of shareholders whose shares have not been bought to require the offeror to buy them out

- The Panel on Takeovers and Mergers is responsible for the regulation of takeovers of public companies

****

Chapter 7

Companies in Trouble

Directors

Directors are appointed individually for a period specified in the articles of association. As stated, public companies must have at least two directors whereas private companies must have one. A director need not be a member of a company and another company may be a director but a company must have at least one director who is a natural person (CA 2006 s 155).

Disqualification of directors

A Director should be aged at least 16 but there is no maximum age limit (CA 2006 s 157). A person must not, without leave of court act as a director or be concerned in the promotion, formation or management of a company if he/she:

a) is an undischarged bankrupt (Company Directors Disqualification Act 1986 s 11)

b) has failed to pay under a county court administration order (CDDA 1986 s 12) or

c) is the subject of a disqualification order.

Relevant factors for CDDA 1986 s 6 include deception, non-payment of crown debts, trading at the risk of creditors and failure to ensure proper financial accounting.

Consequences of contravention

If a person acts while disqualified under the CDDA 1986 provisions, he and the company are criminally liable (CDDA 1986 ss 13-14)

Joint and several liability with the company for the debts of the company is incurred by:

a) a person who acts while disqualified by a disqualification order or whilst he is an undischarged bankrupt, and

b) a person involved in the management of the company who acts on the instructions of (a) without the courts leave (CDDA 1986 s 15)

A court's powers to make a compensation order in criminal cases will be restricted by its decision to disqualify a director (which reduces its means to pay such compensation).

Overcoming disqualification

A disqualified director may be given permission to act as a director of another company on terms specified. Failure to comply with conditions imposed exposes the director to personal liability (Re Brian Sheridan cars (1995)). The length of disqualification is at the judge's discretion. A disqualified person may apply to become a director of a particular company (CDDA 1986 s 17). The court must balance the reasons for disqualification and the risks to the public against the need for the applicant to be a director of a relevant company (Re Barings (No 4) (1998).

Office holders-Insolvency Practitioners

A liquidator, provisional liquidator, administrator, administrative receiver or supervisor of a voluntary arrangement approved by a company under the IA 1986 Pt 1 must, subject to criminal penalties, be a qualified insolvency practitioner or authorized substitute (IA 1986 ss 388-389A). An insolvency practitioner must be an individual authorized by a competent professional body.

Receivers

Debentures often expressly provide that a receiver may be appointed on the occurrence of a specified event rendering the security enforceable. Receivers may also be appointed under an implied power or the court's inherent power. A receiver must generally get in the assets charged and collect any income due on them. He may realize the assets and pay the proceeds in reduction of the amount owed to the debenture holders. He may also petition for liquidation.

Usually it will be better for a company to continue trading and to appoint a receiver as manager of the company as well. A receiver and manager of the whole of the company's property (unless there is another receiver of part) appointed by debenture holders with a floating charge is an administrative receiver with full powers of management and dealing with the company's property. The appointment of a receiver and manager out of court does not automatically terminate the employment of directors or even prevent them from continuing to act, as long as it is not inconsistent with the powers of the receiver and the interests of the debenture holders. (Newhart v Co-operative Bank (1978)).

A receiver appointed by the court is an officer of the court and a receiver appointed by debenture holders is, in principle, their agent. A receiver is not personally bound by the company's existing contracts. However, he and the company are both liable on contracts made by him although an indemnity may be claimed from the company (IA 1986 ss 37 and 44). He owes a duty to all encumbrancers to act in good faith to preserve and realize assets but is not in breach merely because action in the best interests of his debenture holders diminishes the security of subsequent encumbrancers (Downsview Nominees v First City Corp (1992)).

Company administration

Under IA 1986 s.8 and Sch.7 an administrator may be appointed by the court, the holder of a floating charge, or the company or its directors, in order (in descending order of importance):

- to rescue the company as a going concern
- to achieve a better result for its creditors as a whole than would be likely on liquidation; and/or
- to realize property to make a distribution to secured creditors

Administration orders

The court has the power to make an administration order if:

- the company is or is likely to become unable to pay its debts; and
- the order would be reasonably likely to achieve the purpose of administration.

Effect of administration

The effect of administration is that no steps may be taken with a view to winding up, there may not be in office an administrative receiver (if administration order is in effect) or receiver (if the administrator decides). In addition there is a moratorium, that is that the consent of the administrator or permission of the court is necessary for:

1) the enforcement of security, the repossession of hire-purchase goods or a landlords exercise of his right of forfeiture; or

2) enforcement of legal proceedings.

The administrator's duties

The administrator must:

a) notify the company, discoverable creditors and the registrar of and publicise his appointment;

b) obtain a statement of the companies affairs;

c) state his proposals for achieving the purposes of the administration;

d) arrange creditors meeting;

e) take control of company property;

f) manage the company's affairs, business and property in accordance with approved proposals for achieving the purposes of the administration;

g) comply with court directions;

h) take reasonable care to obtain the best price for property disposed of;

i) report on the conclusion of the administration.

Administrators powers

The administrator may:

a) do anything for the management of the affairs, business and property of the company;

b) call meetings of members or creditors;

c) apply to the court for directions;

d) make a distribution to creditors;

e) dispose of charged property (subject to preservation of secured creditors rights); and

f) if sanctioned by the court, dispose of goods subject to a hire purchase agreement (subject to paying the owner of the goods).

Discharge of administrator

The administrator is discharged from office on resignation, removal by the court, ceasing to be qualified as an insolvency practitioner, or discharge of the administration order.

Company voluntary arrangements

The company voluntary arrangement is an important, but much underused, rescue procedure that basically allows the company to enter into a binding arrangement with its creditors. A CVA involves a number of stages:

- A proposal for an arrangement must be made that will form the basis of the CVA. If the company is in administration, the administrator will make the proposal. If it is in liquidation, the liquidator will make the proposal. In all other cases, the directors will make the proposal. Note that creditors and members cannot create and submit a proposal.

- If approved the arrangement will need to be supervised. If an administrator or liquidator made the proposal, he can supervise the arrangement. If the directors made the proposal, a nominee will need to be appointed to supervise the arrangement.

- The nominee must submit a report stating whether the proposed CVA has a reasonable prospect of being approved and implemented and whether or not meetings of the company and its creditors should be convened to consider the proposal.

- If the nominee recommends that such meetings should be called, they should be called in order to approve the proposal. In the event of the meetings reaching conflicting decisions, the decision of the creditors meeting will prevail.

- If the proposal is approved, it will bind the company and will be supervised by the nominee.

Liquidations

Although the winding up of a company (or liquidation) may be carried out in cases other than insolvency, the main statutory provisions are consolidated in the Insolvency Act 1986. Liquidation may be either compulsory or voluntary.

Compulsory liquidation

The court may be petitioned for compulsory liquidation by:

- the company

- any creditor who establishes a prima facie case;
- contributories (those shareholders who may contribute to
- the company's assets on liquidation;
- the Secretary of State; or
- The Official Receiver.

The grounds are that:

a) the company has so resolved;

b) it was incorporated as a public company and has not been issued with a trading certificate within 12 months of registration;

c) it is an "old public company" (i.e. one that has not reregistered as a public company or become a private company under the current legislation;

d) it has not commenced business within a year of incorporation or has not carried on business for a year;

e) the number of members has fallen below the statutory minimum;

f) it is unable to pay its debts; or

g) it is just and equitable to wind it up (IA 1986 s.122).

An order is made if the real purpose of the application is other than for winding up, e.g. to enforce a debt. The "just and equitable" ground enables the court to subject the exercise of legal rights to equitable considerations. It can take account of personal relationships of mutual trust and confidence in small companies, particularly where there is a breach of understanding that all members may participate in the business.

One case that illustrates this is Ebrahimi v Westbourne Galleries (1972) where two partners turned their partnership into a company of which they were equal shareholders and partners until the son of one of them joined the company as a shareholder and director. In time, after a disagreement, the father and son removed the other director from the board. It was held that he was entitled to relief by means of an order to have the company wound up on the "just and equitable" ground.

An order may be similarly made where the majority deprive the minority of their right to appoint and remove their own director.

Once liquidation begins, generally when the petition is presented (IA 1986 s.129) dispositions of company property generally become void (IA 1986 s.127) and litigation involving the company is generally restrained (IA 1986 s.130). The court may dismiss the petition or make a winding up order (IA 1986 s.125). It can do so if the petitioner unreasonably refrains from an alternative course of action. It is empowered to appoint an official receiver and one or more liquidators and has general powers to enable rights and liabilities of claimants and contributories to be settled. Separate meetings of creditors and contributories may decide to nominate a person for the appointment of liquidator.

Voluntary liquidation

The process of voluntary liquidation begins when the company so resolves, from which point it generally ceases to carry on business (IA 1986 ss.84-88). If the directors of the company have previously made a declaration of the company's solvency, it is a member's voluntary winding up (IA 1986 s.90). In that case the general meeting appoints the liquidators. If not it is a creditors voluntary winding up (IA 1986 s.90). If this is so then a meeting of creditors must be called, to which the directors must report on the company's affairs (IA 1986 ss. 98-99).

In the case of a members voluntary winding up, a liquidator must be appointed (IA 1986 s.91). In the case of a creditors voluntary winding up, a liquidator and a liquidation committee may be appointed (IA 1986 ss.100-101). Though a voluntary winding up of a company has begun, a compulsory liquidation order is still possible, but a petitioning contributory would need to satisfy the court that a voluntary liquidation would prejudice the contributories (IA 1986 s.116).

Powers and duties of liquidators

The powers available to a liquidator during a wind up of a company are contained within IA 1986 Sch.4. Certain powers are exercisable without sanction whilst others require sanction. This will be either by a court or by an extraordinary resolution (in a members voluntary winding up) or the liquidation committee or a meeting of the companies creditors (in a creditors voluntary winding up) (IA 1986 ss.165-168.

With sanctions, the liquidator may pay creditors and make compromises or arrangements with creditors. Without sanctions the liquidator may carry on legal proceedings and carry on the business of the company so far as necessary for its beneficial winding up. The liquidator can sell property, claim against insolvent contributories, raise money on the security of company assets and do anything else deemed necessary for the company's winding up and distribution of assets. In a compulsory liquidation, the liquidator must assume control of all property to which the company seems to be entitled. The exercise of his powers is subject to the supervision of the courts.

In a voluntary winding up, the liquidator may exercise the courts power of settling a list of contributories and of making calls and he may summon general meetings of the company for any purpose he thinks fit (IA 1986 s.165). In a creditor's voluntary winding up he must report to the creditor meeting on the exercise of his powers (IA 1986 s.166). T

The liquidator owes a fiduciary duty to the company and should investigate the causes of the company's failure and the conduct of its managers. Depending upon the type of liquidation he may be removed by the court, by a general meeting of the members or by a general meeting of the creditors.

Under IA 1986 s.108(2) the court may remove a liquidator and appoint another if there is a "cause shown" by the applicant for his removal and why this should be done.

Priority of claims

Before claims are met, creditors are entitled to enforce their secured claims against company property subject to fixed charges to the extent their claims may be so met: thereafter they rank as unsecured creditors. The costs of liquidation must first be met out of the company's remaining assets.

Next in the queue are certain preferential payments such as occupational pension contributions and remuneration owed to employees for the preceding four months and accrued holiday remuneration.

Claims of persons who have distrained goods within the preceding three months are postponed to the preferential creditors (IA 1986 s.176). A prescribed part of the company's net property must usually be available to satisfy the claims of unsecured creditors. The expenses of winding up must be paid before the claims of floating charges are satisfied. The unsecured creditors fund is: 50% of property worth up to £10,000 and 20% of further property up to a maximum of £600,000. Following this, the claims of debenture holders secured by floating charges are paid (IA 1986 ss.40-175).

Remaining unsecured claims provable in insolvency are then paid *pari passu.* This includes claims qua purchasers of shares by claimants who have become members.

All remaining debts are then paid. Finally, the company's assets are divided amongst the members according to their rights (in the articles) on liquidation. No provision is necessary for untraced shareholders. Unclaimed assets vest in the Crown as *bona vacantia* (CA 2006 s.1012).

Dissolution

When the company's affairs are wound up, the liquidator must call a final meeting of the members or the creditors or both to which he has to report on the winding up. Within one week of the meeting prior to dissolution after a voluntary winding up, the liquidator must send to the Registrar a copy of his accounts and make a return to him of the holding of the meeting. The company is dissolved three months after such registration. In the case of a compulsory winding up, he must notify the court and the Registrar of the holding and results of the meeting. The company can then be dissolved.

However, an application can be made to the court for registration to the register (CA 2006 ss.1029-1034). This will enable the completion of any unfinished business.

Striking off the register

Less expensive than liquidation or formal dissolution is an application to the Registrar for the company to be struck of the register. The liquidator may do this if he has reasonable cause to believe that the company is not carrying on business or has been wound up (CA 2006 ss. 1000-1011).

Misconduct

Adjustment of prior transaction

Where (between the presentation of a petition and the making of an order for administration, or at such relevant time as is noted below) a company, within two years of the onset of insolvency, has entered into a transaction at an undervalue to the company or given a preference to a person connected to the company or, within six months of the onset of insolvency, has given a preference to a third party, then, on the application of an administrator or liquidator, the court may make an order restoring the position (IA 1986 ss.238-241). The court may also grant relief against extortionate credit transactions entered within three years of an administration order or liquidation (IA 1986 s.244).

Wrongful or fraudulent trading

It is an offence for a person to be involved in trading by a company to defraud creditors (CA 2006 s.993). If, during liquidation, it appears that any business of the company has been carried on for any fraudulent purpose, on the application of the liquidator the court may declare those involved to make such contribution to the company's assets as it thinks proper (IA 1986 s.213) to compensate for the loss caused. Liability under this section can also be extended to third parties whose knowledge effectively constitutes corporate knowledge.

A director of a company who is aware of impending liquidation may also be made liable to make such payment as the court thinks fit. Criminal liability can be imposed for certain offences in connection with liquidations. (IA 1986 ss.218 and 432).

Takeovers Reconstructions and Amalgamations
Schemes of Arrangements
Sections 895-899 of the CA 2006 provide for schemes of arrangement. A scheme of arrangement would be made between a company and its creditors or members. The provisions are usually utilized where there is an internal reconstruction. The procedure involves application to the court with the proposed plan. If the propose plan is legal, then the court would order meetings of the members and creditors as appropriate. If the meetings give the required consent by 75% in value of shares or debts, then this is reported back to the court which will then sanction the scheme if satisfied that the required consent is given.

Amalgamation

A procedure for merger is offered by the IA s. 986 where a company goes into voluntary liquidation. The liquidator may accept shares from a transferee company in exchange for assets of the company. The shares of the transferee company are then distributed to the former members of the transferor company.

Takeover

The procedure for a takeover is provided for by Part X111A of the CA 1985. Where a takeover involves a quoted company, the Code on Takeover and Mergers is the most crucial document. The Code is made up of general principles and detailed rules governing the conduct of takeovers. Under the Financial Services and Markets Act 2000, the Financial Services Authority has endorsed the Code and has the power to take enforcement action against parties in breach of the code if so requested by the panel. Part X111A also provides for the compulsory acquisition of shares where the offeror acquires 90% of the shares of a target company. The acquisition of the minority holding will be ordered on the same terms as the majority was acquired. Not only does the majority have the right to acquire the minority, but the minority has a corresponding right to be acquired.

The law has been restated in accordance with the EU Directive on Takeover Bids (2004). The Code on Takeovers and Mergers has been placed within a statutory framework. Sections 942-946 of the

CA 2006 give the panel wide powers and responsibilities. The courts will be able to judicially review the panel.

****

Glossary of terms

Agent. A person engaged to act on behalf of another person (that other person being known as the principal).

Articles of association. The principle constitutional document of a company that provides the rules that regulate the internal affairs of the company.

Authorised share capital. The maximum total nominal value of shares that mat be issued by a company.

Called-up share capital. Where a company calls for payment on shares that have not been fully paid for, the amount called for plus the paid up share capital is known as the called-up share capital.

Capacity. The ability of a person to enter into certain transactions or make certain decisions. For example, a party's contractual capacity refers to his ability to enter into legally binding contracts.

Charge. Any form of security where possession of property is not transferred.

Class rights. The class rights that are attached to different classes of shares.

Companies House. An executive agency of government responsible for incorporating and dissolving companies, and for storing information relating to companies which can be inspected by the public.

Company secretary. An officer and agent of the company who is usually responsible for ensuring that the company complies with its legal and financial obligations.

Corporate personality. The separate personality that belongs to legal persons (e.g. companies).

Debenture. A document whereby a company creates or acknowledges a debt, whether secured or unsecured.

Debt capital. The capital that companies obtain through borrowing from others. Also known as 'loan capital'.

Dividend. The distribution, usually in cash, of profits to shareholders, usually at a fixed amount per share.

Fiduciary. The word 'fiduciary' can refer to:
1) a relationship of trust and confidence, or
2) a person who is in such a relationship and who is

under an obligation to act in the other's interests (for example, a doctor, solicitor or trustee).

Incorporation. The process by which a company or limited liability partnership is created.

Insolvency. A company is deemed to be insolvent if it is unable to pay it's debts as they fall due.

Issued share capital. The total nominal vale of shares that a company has actually issued.

Joint and several liability. Persons who are jointly and severally liable, may be sued jointly for a loss, or any one person can be sued for the entire loss.

Limited liability partnership. A business structure established by the Limited Liability Partnerships Act 2000.

Listed company. A public company whose shares are listed on a stock exchange.

Memorandum of association. Historically, the principal constitutional document which regulated the external affairs of a company. Its importance has diminished significantly following the passing of the 2006 Companies Act.

Nominal value. A fixed value attached to shares, which may bear no resemblance to the actual value of the shares.

Ordinary resolution. A resolution passed by an ordinary majority.

Ordinary shares. Where a company only has one class of shares, its shares will be known as ordinary shares, which will entitle the holder to the normal rights of share ownership (e.g. to vote at general meetings).

Paid-up share capital. The combined nominal value of share capital that has actually been paid.

Parent company. A company is a parent company of another company if it:

1) holds the majority of voting rights in the other company, or
2) is a member of the other company and has the right to remove or appoint the board of directors, or
3) is a member of the other company and controls alone,

136

pursuant to an agreement with other members, a majority of the voting rights in it.

Partnership. A business structure defined by the Partnership Act 1890 s1(1) as 'the relation which subsists between persons carrying on a business in common with a view to profit.

Pre-emption rights. The right of first refusal belonging to existing shareholders upon the allotment of a new batch of shares. The company must first offer the shares to the existing shareholders.

Preference shares. Shares which entitle the holder to some sort of benefit or enhanced right, usually in relation to the entitlement to a dividend.

Promoter. A person who undertakes and enters into the process of setting up a company.

Proxy. A person appointed to vote for another (e.g. at a general meeting of a company)

Quorum. The minimum number of persons required to have a formal meeting.

Redeemable shares. Shares issued by a company which can be bought back (redeemed) by that company should the company or the member so require, or upon the passing of a stated period.

Registered company. A company created through incorporation by registration.

Registrar of Companies. The Chief Executive of Companies House. The principal functions of the Registrar are to register the incorporation and dissolution of companies, and to ensure that documents delivered to Companies House are accurate.

Resolution. A decision arrived at by a formal vote.

Share. A measure of a person's interest in a company. The owner of a share is called a shareholder.

Share capital. The capital that the company acquires through the selling of shares. Also known as equity capital.

Share premium. The sum paid for a share in excess of the shares nominal value, which usually represents the difference between the nominal value of the share and its market value.

Sole proprietorship. A business structure consisting of an individual who conducts business on his own account and who bears the risk of business failure and is also entitled to the profits of the business.

Sole trader. A sole proprietor who is not a professional.

Special resolution. A resolution passed by a majority of no less than 75 per cent.

Subsidiary. A company is a subsidiary company of another company, if that other company:

1) holds the majority of voting rights in it, or
2) is a member of it and has the right to remove or appoint the board of directors, or
3) is a member of it and controls alone, pursuant to an agreement with other members, a majority of the voting rights in it.

Unregistered company. A company not incorporated by registration.

****

Index

****

www.straightforwardco.co.uk

All titles, listed below, in the Straightforward Guides Series can be purchased online, using credit card or other forms of payment by going to www.straightfowardco.co.uk A discount of 25% per title is offered with online purchases.

Law
A Straightforward Guide to:
Consumer Rights
Bankruptcy Insolvency and the Law
Employment Law
Private Tenants Rights
Family law
Small Claims in the County Court
Contract law
Intellectual Property and the law
Divorce and the law
Leaseholders Rights
The Process of Conveyancing
Knowing Your Rights and Using the Courts
Producing Your own Will
Housing Rights
The Bailiff the law and You

Probate and The Law

Company law

What to Expect When You Go to Court

Guide to Competition Law

Give me Your Money-Guide to Effective Debt Collection

General titles

Letting Property for Profit

Buying, Selling and Renting property

Buying a Home in England and France

Bookkeeping and Accounts for Small Business

Creative Writing

Freelance Writing

Writing Your own Life Story

Writing performance Poetry

Writing Romantic Fiction

Speech Writing

Teaching Your Child to Read and write

Teaching Your Child to Swim

Raising a Child-The Early Years

Creating a Successful Commercial Website

The Straightforward Business Plan

The Straightforward C.V.

Successful Public Speaking

Handling Bereavement

Play the Game-A Compendium of Rules

Individual and Personal Finance

Understanding Mental Illness

The Two Minute Message

Guide to Self Defence

Buying a Used Car

Tiling for Beginners

Go to: www.straightforwardco.co.uk